Praise for J
and TALK BIG

"*Talk Big: How to Interview Celebrities and Make Them Love You!* will appeal to anyone charged with interviewing big names from any field, for any purpose. It surveys the discussion process with an eye to identifying and overcoming obstacles common to interviewing success."

—D. Donovan, Senior Reviewer, *Midwest Book Review*

"*Talk Big* is a fun, compulsive read packed with interesting--and often hilarious--tips about how to interview famous people. But it's so much more than that. At its heart, this book is about character, confidence, and courage. It's about letting yourself off the hook for dreaming big, and it's about having the guts to pursue what might seem out of your reach. Do yourself a favor and settle into John Kerwin's head for a little while. You'll come out a better person."

—Patrick Ryan, author of *The Dream Life of Astronauts*

"John Kerwin's book is essential for podcasters and hosts on the how-to's on interviewing big shots. Don't get nervous, get this book."

—Judy Carter, author of *The Message of You, The New Comedy Bible*

"John has what is so necessary to be a good interviewer and that is, supreme confidence. What it also shows, which is another thing a good interviewer can use, is the man's got chutzpah. Without confidence, chutzpah, and preparation, you're just spinning your wheels. And John Kerwin is, as indicated in *Talk Big*, prepared to meet these celebrities head on."

—Lawrence Grobel, *The Art of the Interview*, and *You, Talking to Me*

"John was so bright, witty, and he made the entire show so fun that I watched it from the audience."

—Steve Wozniak, co-founder of Apple®

"It was nothing but fun! He's "got it" – no doubt about it."

—David Carradine (*Kung Fu, Kill Bill*), Emmy Award nominee and 4-time Golden Globe® Award nominee

"He's fresh and new and fun and delightful. Amazingly sexy! Watch out Conan!"

—Cloris Leachman, Oscar-winning actress and 8-time Emmy Award®-winner

"I had a thoroughly enjoyable time. I think John is very good at this, he's very funny, and he has a nice sense of how to play with the conventions of the talk show."

—Tom Bergeron, 2-time Emmy Award-winner and 13 time nominee; host of *Dancing with the Stars*

"John is a strong host . . . very personable and interested. He is not trying to be interesting . . . he's genuinely interested. He's funny . . . charming."

—Nancy Cartwright, Emmy Award-winning actress and voice of Bart Simpson

"I thought the show was great. I was really surprised with how intimate it was."

—Brian McKnight,16-time Grammy Award®-nominated musician

"John is a great host...he made me feel listened to instead of just wanting to get to the next question. I felt very comfortable. I had a wonderful time... I would do the show again."

—Melissa Manchester, Grammy Award-winning singer (*Midnight Blue* and *Don't Cry Out Loud*)

"John was phenomenal and I enjoyed myself immensely. I would definitely come back on the show if ever asked. He was hilarious and made me feel comfortable and at ease. He really works great with the guests and is very generous."

—Antonio Sabato, Jr. (*General Hospital, Melrose Place*)

"He's nice and funny, usually I'm nervous about these things, but I was comfortable once it started."

—Michael Dorn, (Worf in the *Star Trek* franchise)

"John is a genuine and very warm host. He was engaged with me even during the breaks, which was very refreshing. I connected with him from the very beginning."

—Eriq La Salle *(ER, Coming to America, Jacob's Ladder)*

"It was a great deal of fun. John is very relaxed, free and easy. A very funny, decent, likeable guy."

—Michael Gross, *(Family Ties, Tremors)*

"John is not your ordinary John. He's an extraordinary Kerwin! I will come back for another interview whenever he wants!"

—Eric Roberts, *(Star 80, The Pope of Greenwich Village, Runaway Train)*

"I think he was very generous and lovely. He let me shoot my mouth off and he didn't snap me into "his mode"; he allowed me free reign. He trusted me enough and gave me great respect."

—Ed Asner, 7-time Emmy Award-winning actor, *(The Mary Tyler Moore Show, Lou Grant, Up)*

"The show was a lot of fun. John is a very funny and sweet man, just like talking to a friend."

—Dee Wallace *(E.T. the Extra-Terrestrial, Cujo, The Howling)*

"It was my honor to be with the Great John Kerwin! Could not have been more fun."

—Robert Forster *(Jackie Brown, The Delta Force, Breaking Bad)*

"I found him very personable; very easy to talk to. He made it fun. He can draw the people in; get them interested in his guest, and him."

—Gloria Gaynor, Two-time Grammy Award-winning musician, singer of *I Will Survive*

"John is very funny, very kind and extremely charming. I really had a good time. He made me feel at home, and there was a good chemistry. I felt I could say or do whatever I wanted. I would like to come back because of how he made me feel."

—Bai Ling *(The Crow, Red Corner, Crank: High Voltage)*

"Pleasant! Very pleasant, and he's real -- a lot of hosts are plastic and fake, but he's very real."

—Sean Young *(Blade Runner, Dune, Ace Ventura, Pet Detective)*

"John was a great host. I really enjoyed myself and I can see John going places."

—Louis Gossett Jr., Academy Award-winning actor *(An Officer and a Gentleman)*; Emmy Award-winner, *(Roots)*

"He's very genuine; he allows you to express thoughts and ideas instead of just buzz clips. If we had a beer, it would have felt like I was hangin' out with one of my buds."

—Zack Ward (*A Christmas Story, Titus)*

"John is very facile. He's got a real touch and he made me feel comfortable."

—Steven Bauer (*Scarface, Traffic, Primal Fear*)

"He wasn't 'trying too hard' and he made me feel comfortable. And while some of his questions were bold, he's one of the few who didn't make me feel pressured. He made me feel like I was doing a good job."

—Amber Smith *(Playboy, The Mirror Has Two Faces, American Beauty)*

"It was a lot of fun...great experience...very professional. I would recommend John to people I know. He's very likeable, very nice, and I felt very comfortable...great host...kept it moving which is what a good host should do."

—Maz Jobrani, Comedian (Showtime's *Brown and Friendly, I Come in Peace)*

"John is the nicest man; he's adorable, he's darling. You can tell that he's an affectionate and warm-hearted person. He's also lighthearted and allows a performer to do whatever they want. It's a wonderful experience."

—Karen Black *(Five Easy Pieces, Easy Rider, Airport, Nashville)*

"He's genuine and it really shows through. He's accessible, he's funny, and he's sexy."

—Alexandra Paul *(Baywatch,* Stephen King's *Christine)*

"John is a treat. It was a lot of fun, easy and wonderful. He made me feel very comfortable and I felt like he was genuinely interested in knowing about me and what I'm doing. Seemed to be genuinely interested in my film and my company."

—Connie Stevens ***(Hawaiian Eye, Rock-A-Bye Baby, Grease 2)***

"I had a great time; John is very approachable and likable. He lets his guests talk without interrupting them. He doesn't have an ego like a lot of other talk show hosts. I would definitely come back again."

—Maria Conchita Alonso ***(Moscow on the Hudson, The Running Man)***

"John's a great host! He made me quite comfortable. He definitely has a feel for what's going on – he's a natural."

—Adrianne Curry ***(America's Next Top Model, My Fair Brady)***

"He really lets you play. He's fun to play with, and that makes him charming. He's got a wonderful looseness."

—Henry Jaglom, Film Director ***(Someone to Love, Can She Bake a Cherry Pie?)***

"John's a very good host, he's quick and has good give and take. Being on the show was very cool, I felt completely relaxed and had a lot of fun."

—Ally Walker (***The Profiler, While You Were Sleeping, Universal Soldier)***

"I know there's big things in store for him – I can see myself lying in bed late at night and watching him."

—Luenell ***(Dolemite is My Name, Borat, Taken 2, That's My Boy)***

"He's great. It was a pleasure. He's sharp, very cordial; very easy to open up to."

— Kelly LeBrock (***Weird Science, The Woman in Red, Hard to Kill)***

"Great! A great and gracious host, with a warm, involved audience. I had a great time! He really talks to you, and not at you, and is able to make you relax. You end up feeling free and able to talk."

—Robert Gossett ***(The Closer, Major Crimes)***

"I had such a great time and John was a super fun host. I was shown great hospitality from John and the whole crew from the moment I arrived. The greatest show!"

—Carmit Bachar (original member of *The Pussycat Dolls*)

"John is hysterical. And I was sad when the interview was over. I wanted to keep talking to him."

—Nikki Ziering *(Austin Powers in Goldmember, American Wedding)*

"I had a lot of fun. It was easy to bounce back and forth with John."

—Jayde Nicole *(The Hills, Holly's World,* Former *Playboy Playmate of the Year)*

"I used to see him up at the Improv. He's a clever, personable guy who knows how to interview people — a skill not evident in everyone who's ever starred in a talk show. He does this with no pre-interviews or semi-scripted exchanges...you know, the way talk shows used to be."

—Mark Evanier, Author, Comics historian, Blogger: *News from Me*

"John is a very warm person. He's funny, and was really good to bounce off of; he knew when to lay off and let me talk. Some talk show hosts get their lines in -- he had good timing. With dancing, everything is about timing -- and it's the same with interviewing."

—Corky Ballas *(Dancing with the Stars)*

"John was wonderful. He was very easy to talk to and so funny."

—Jackie Christie *(Basketball Wives LA)*

"I enjoyed talking with him very much. And he seemed to be extremely respectful and generous to me and I appreciated that, so it was a good experience for me to share with him. (He's) somebody I would follow. I'm so pleased I got to know him."

—Elliott Gould *(Ocean's 11, M*A*S*H, The Long Goodbye, Bob & Carol & Ted & Alice)*

TALK BIG

How to Interview Celebrities
and Make Them Love You!

JOHN KERWIN

QB PUBLISHING

ISBN: 978-1-7345062-0-4 (Paperback)

E-ISBN: 978-1-7345062-1-1 (E-book)

This is a work of creative nonfiction. Some portions have been fictionalized in varying degrees, for various purposes.

Published 2022 First edition

Library of Congress Control Number: 2020904277

Cover design by Pete Garceau

Editor: Alan Roberts

Photographs by:

Lucie Aleks: www.luciealeks.com

George Kritikos: www.afterfx.com

Don Sweeney

Stacy Altman

For information: www.johnkerwin.com

Library of Congress Cataloging-in-Publication Data

Kerwin, John, author.

Talk Big: How to Interview Celebrities and Make Them Love You / John Kerwin.

Includes bibliographical references and index. | Hollywood, CA: QB Publishing, 2022.

LCCN: 2020904277 | ISBN: 978-1-7345062-0-4 (pbk.) | 978-1-7345062-1-1 (ebook)

LCSH Interviewing--Methodology. | Interviewing--Technique. | Interviewing in mass media. | Interviewing in journalism. | Mass media--Authorship. | Webcasting--Handbooks, manuals, etc. | Communication. | Interpersonal relations. | Celebrities. | Arts--Press coverage. | BISAC LANGUAGE ARTS & DISCIPLINES / Journalism | PERFORMING ARTS / General

LCC PN4784.I6 .K47 2021 | DDC 070.4/3--dc23

Printed in the United States of America

ACKNOWLEDGMENTS

To Alan Roberts, the handsomest editor in the business. He also edited this section.

Thanks to my cover designer, Pete Garceau, who suffered through my idiotic suggestions such as, *"Can we use the font from the Ba• Motherfucker wallet in Pulp Fiction?"*

To my still photographers, Lucie Aleks and George Kritikos. Thank you for the fine pictures featured in this book. And thanks for using every Photoshop trick to make me look better.

I'm grateful to one of my longtime comedy writers, Tony DeSena, who gave terrific suggestions for this book. After many years writing for *The Tonight Show Starring Johnny Carson* and *Late Night with Davi• Letterman,* Tony finally hit the big time, working on my show.

Thank you to Stephanie Hicks for her wonderful suggestions and constant reminders to keep the book "current." In the first draft I wrote, *"In my opinion, at the burning bush, Moses was interviewing Go•."* I replaced that with an anecdote about PewDiePie.

My longtime friends Steve Rosinski, Sunday Theodore, and Ilene Sanders, who miss the days when they could tell me, "I can't talk anymore, I'm running out of minutes."

Finally, to my father, who in my 6th grade graduation book wrote:

When you grow ol•er
An• no longer a la•
Think of ole •a•
An• the fun we ha•

To my mother.

The first book I remember was one my mother
read to me on a rainy night called *Rainbows.*

I was a little boy and I loved having her read to me. By the
time she was finished, I had learned all about rainbows.

I asked, *"It's raining outsi•e.*
Do you think we coul• see a rainbow now?"

"I •on't know. Let's see," she said.

She took me to the window, and in one of the most
magical moments of my life, I saw a rainbow.

It was the prettiest thing I'd ever seen. And it showed me that
sometimes... things you read about in books can come true.

Contents

INTERVIEW CATEGORIES 25

GETTING THE INTERVIEW 43

PREPARATION 63

CONDUCTING YOUR INTERVIEW 87

MY "ROCKY" START

Visiting my aunt in Los Angeles, I'm a seventeen-year-old with a dream—interviewing my hero, Sylvester Stallone.

I call Stallone's manager and when I finally get him on the phone he says, "Kid, Sylvester Stallone is the number one box office star in the world. Everyone wants to interview him. I'm his manager and I only met him twice. Some things in life are impossible. This is one of 'em."

So I call his agent, who has an even shorter answer:

CLICK.

Welcome to Show Business.

The next day I'm in Hollywood and I see a man selling maps to the star's homes for five bucks. I ask, "Excuse me, do you have Sylvester Stallone's address in there?"

He says, "Oh YEAH! Stallone's in here."

"Well I *really* want to buy that!"

"Twenty bucks."

The map indicates Stallone lives on Amalfi Drive in Pacific Palisades. I decide to go there... it's Thanksgiving Day.

I take three buses from my aunt's house, followed by a long walk. I hike up to the address and see a house out of a fairy tale. Cartoon bluebirds should be circling it. I press the intercom. A polite voice says, "How may I help you?"

"Hi, I'd like to see Sylvester Stallone for an interview."

Moments later the voice says, "I'm sorry, he's not here. He's out of town."

"Okay, thank you."

But I stick around.

After a while, cars start arriving filled with families. Someone's hosting a Thanksgiving dinner, and as the families pass by, I blurt out, "Welcome! Happy Thanksgiving!"

They look at me like I'm Norman Bates.

Ten minutes later, the police arrive. One of the cops walks up to me and says, "What are ya doin' here?"

I say, "I want to interview Sylvester Stallone."

"Not gonna happen. C'mon, let's go."

"I'm not leaving."

"Would you like to be arrested?" He asks, while taking out a pair of handcuffs.

At that moment, who walks out of the house wearing karate pants and a T-shirt? That's right, Sylvester Stallone! He's flanked by a couple of scary-looking bodyguards, who are definitely not in the holiday spirit.

Stallone walks right up to me, and in his signature baritone says, "What can I do for you?"

I nervously answer, "Very nice to meet you, Mr. Stallone. My name is John Kerwin, and I would like to interview you."

He says, "Why don't you go to Barbara Streisand's house and bother her?"

Everyone laughs, including the cops. I say, "I did, but she has better security."

No one laughs at that.

Regaining my nerve, I say, "I'm here on Thanksgiving because in *Rocky*, my favorite moment is when Adrian says, 'It's Thanksgiving' and you say, 'To you it's Thanksgiving, to me it's Thursday.' Coming from a broken family, I related to that."

Stallone says, "How old are you?"

"Seventeen."

He whispers something to one of his bodyguards.

I quickly change the subject and say, "I really want to be successful. Can you give me some advice?"

He pauses, thinks for a moment and says, "Whatever you do, never give up on your dreams. I remember being so poor I could barely eat. In fact, it got so bad, I had to sell my dog to get food. But I never gave up and when things finally got better, the first thing I did was buy my dog back. And he was my dog Butkus in *Rocky*."

"How close were you to quitting?"

"There was no quitting. Nothing was going to make me give up on my dream."

He then says, "Now I have a question for you. What are you really doing here right now?"

"It's my dream to interview *you.*"

He looks me and says, "Well you just did."

At that moment, his bodyguard comes out of the house carrying Thanksgiving to-go bags for me and the police officers.

I say, "Thank you, Mr. Stallone!" and we shake hands. As he walks back to the house, in my toughest voice, I yell, "HEY ROCKY!"

He turns around and yells back, "YO!"

I say, "Happy Thursday."

He smiles and says, "Happy Thursday."

Since that defining moment, I've interviewed over five hundred celebrities.

That's the day I learned the most valuable lesson of my life. No matter what the obstacles, never give up on your dreams.

INTRODUCTION

Comedian and talk show host Bill Maher has a stand-up special called *The Golden Goose.* The special's theme is that the golden goose is where all good things come from. In Bill's case, it's stand-up comedy. For me, the golden goose is interviewing celebrities. They've provided my greatest moments, my greatest loves, my best friends, and my purpose in life. The purpose of this book is to share with you what I've learned over a seventeen-year career, and guide you down the path of excitement, passion, and creative fulfilment.

With this book you'll receive an insider's knowledge on creating ***compelling*** celebrity interviews via podcasts, YouTube, IG, Twitter, Facebook, TV, radio, print, red carpet interviews, conference and event panels, or whatever new media pops up where stars and influencers are interviewed. Included is a checklist to guide you step-by-step through the interview process. I'll also share the private advice I received from my mentor, Garry Shandling. And I've included the transcript from a television interview I did with David Carradine, along with my comments, to give you a rare insight into the **thought process** that goes into a celebrity interview. There's also a list of 100 celebrity interview questions to help stimulate your mind as you prepare for your specific interviews. If you apply the principles found in these pages, you'll be equipped to interview everyone from Barack Obama to Sponge Bob.

An added benefit is that these techniques are directly transferrable to establishing rapport with "celebrities" in your daily life. That may be the CEO of your company, a new customer, or even someone you want to date. ***TALK BIG Tips*** are included throughout the book to help you powerfully ***connect*** (one of the ***Three C's***) with the essential people in your personal and professional life.

Remember those SNL sketches where Chris Farley played a star-struck interviewer who was so painfully nervous and awkward that he turned every conversation into a train wreck? None of us want our interviews or conversations to end up like that.

My goal in writing this book is to help novice interviewers as well as experienced ones. If you're a beginner, my intent is to give you the guidance needed as you embark on this new journey. The idea is for you to reread this book at different stages of your career, hopefully always picking up something that helps you grow. If you're a veteran, you're probably always striving to improve; to learn more about your craft and utilize new techniques and methods to help advance your work. This book is also for you.

The goal is simple—to guide you toward creating ***compelling*** and enlightening celebrity interviews. Transcend the ordinary by using these tools to reach the height of your potential.

1 UNDERSTANDING CELEBRITIES

What celebrities want is to look amazing. There, I said it. What's important may vary from movie star to online influencer, but I can assure you that every single one of them wants to look beautiful and sound brilliant. They want to know that the lighting, makeup, and audio enable them to look and sound their best. Specifically, they want you to make them better than they actually are.

They want to come across as being highly interesting and funny. For some, it's important that they sound intelligent. For others, it's more important to look tough or cool. Your research will give you clues as to how they specifically want to be represented. And here's the key, you want to achieve that for them like no one else has before.

They want you to be effective in boosting their career and furthering their stardom. Whatever they may be promoting, they want to know you've gone above and beyond in plugging it. They want to watch you being a great salesman, and to do that, you'll sometimes be a greater actor than they are.

But that's not all.

Secretly, they want much more. They want the interview to achieve greatness. I believe they want to feel a ***connection*** and chemistry with you, allowing them to transcend the other hundreds of interviews they've done. They want the interview to feel like a discovery has been made, leaving them with a deeper understanding of themselves, their life, and their art. Like someone who's endured dozens of nightmare dates, they're praying you'll be that special someone in their life.

It's no different than an actor who does four films a year, each time secretly hoping the film they're working on will achieve greatness and demonstrate their talent at the highest possible level.

WHY YOU SHOULD LOVE CELEBRITIES

As an interviewer of famous people, it's essential for you to stay on a celebrity's good side. Why? Because aside from it leading to stronger, more in-depth interviews, celebrities have the power to make a single phone call on your behalf, and that call might change your life. (Or maybe they'll give you a Thanksgiving dinner.) Through strong interviewing, you'll demonstrate a unique skill and make a positive impact on them. You might even become a trusted confidant.

Too often, people seek to expose, vilify, or ambush well-known public figures. Unless your name is Borat, don't do that. Not only is your reputation too important, the truth is, despite appearances celebrities are highly sensitive people. They got into showbiz for multiple reasons, but most of all to feel special. They've made sacrifices that would make a Yorkie's hair curl, and their egos are battered and bruised from hundreds of auditions… and hundreds of rejections. So if a celebrity asks a small favor, such as, "Please don't talk about my divorce," *Don't talk about their divorce!*

Bottom line: You're teaming up to produce a work of art that will live on after both of you have exited the stage.

CELEBRITY INTERVIEWERS WILL ALWAYS BE IN DEMAND

If you went back in time to caveman days, you'd find a brave hunter who killed a beast to fed his entire village. While the villagers gathered around the fire, feasting on this food, someone peppered this hero with questions like,

> "How did you come across this animal?"
>
> "Were you scared?"
>
> "What weapon did you use?"
>
> "How close were you to dying?"
>
> "What's next?"

That was the first celebrity interviewer.

No matter how our culture evolves, there will always be celebrities and those of us who interview them. The definition of a celebrity will change, as we've gone from the caveman Gronk to YouTuber, MrBeast. The media will also be ever-changing, like how we've gone from radio and TV to Zoom interviews during the COVID-19 pandemic. But it's all the same idea. Interesting people will always walk the earth, and an audience wanting to know everything about them will follow.

And that's where *we* come in.

MY "GETAWAY" CAR

People love celebrities. They want to learn everything about them, and thanks to interviews, they often will. People emulate stars, who serve as role models for their fashion choices, workout routines, book selections, and virtually every other aspect of their life. I once watched an interview with Jennifer Aniston where she explained how when she buys a basic t-shirt, she has it tailored so it fits perfectly. And then I *did* that! Yes, it's embarrassing to admit.

The following is a confession that's even worse, a story which I'm hesitant to tell, yet it illuminates our culture of celebrity.

When I was in my early 20's I was strapped for cash. I owned a 1972 White Chevy Impala that was on its last legs. I wanted to sell it, pronto, so I put an ad in the paper for $500. The best offer I got was $175, which I simply couldn't accept.

And the rent was already two weeks late.

That night on TV, I was watching an old Steve McQueen movie called *The Getaway*. I suddenly jolted up as I saw the Hollywood legend driving a car that was the exact same year, make, model, even *color* as mine. The wheels started turning.

The next morning, I went to a cinema collectibles store and bought a mini poster from *The Getaway*, featuring Steve McQueen and the car in the photo. Then I went up into the mountains to see a friend of mine who was a gun enthusiast. I asked him to shoot a few rounds into the back seat of my car, which he gladly did with a .357 Magnum. The next day, a new ad appeared in the paper stating there was a car for sale that was Steve McQueen's Chevy Impala from the film, *The Getaway*.

A few mornings later, my apartment manager woke me up, pounding on my front door.

"There's a line of people around the block who want to buy your car."

I couldn't believe it! People oohed and aahed looking at *The Getaway* poster taped to the car proving its "star status," while marveling at the bullet holes in the back seat. A bidding war began and I ended up selling the car for $11,000. I was so worried about getting busted, I paid my rent and moved that night.

As Bugs Bunny once said, "Ain't I a stinker?"

Point is, people love celebrities and will often go to ridiculous lengths to emulate them. It's why product placement is an eleven billion dollar a year business. It's no accident my Maurice Lacroix wristwatch is the same one Bradley Cooper wore in *The Hangover*. It's also why you'll often hear common celebrity interview questions such as: What do you eat? Fans want to copy their heroes. One of the biggest mistakes I made as a kid was watching *Popeye* cartoons, then asking my mother to cook me spinach.

As you write questions and prepare for your celebrity interviews, remember how that star affects your viewers, and zero in on what about them is valuable to share.

Oh, and if you ever consider buying a car that was featured in a movie, ask for a certificate of authenticity.

WILL COMPUTERS TAKE OVER INTERVIEWING?

The most fascinating episodes of the game show *Jeopar•y* were when past champions, Ken Jennings and Brad Rutter, went up against IBM's computer, Watson. Watson had every fact imaginable installed into its system and it beat Jennings and Rutter, handily. That's because *Jeopar•y*, for the most part, involves having facts readily available.

How can any human compete with that?

However, you could input every conceivable question into Watson and the computer would still be a poor interviewer. Why? Because you create a great interview by ***connecting*** with a guest on a human level. You ask questions based on your own life experiences and why the celebrity resonates with you. The drama of a great interview hinges on your emotions, your sense of humor, and your worldview. Through your questions, reactions and follow-up questions, you expose your heart and mind, and this exposure transfers to the subject, encouraging them to do the same. You may not ask perfect, pre-scripted questions like a computer, but what's far more important is revealing your curiosity, your thoughts, and ultimately, your soul.

2

SECRETS TO BEING A CELEBRITY INTERVIEWER

Ten years ago, I went to the Los Angeles County Museum of Art to see a Salvador Dalí exhibit. His surreal, over-the-top paintings and drawings were curated to command your attention. But in one corner off to the side, a large crowd was gathered. I was wondering which painting it could be, but as it turned out, it wasn't a painting at all. It was a small television showing Dick Cavett interviewing Dalí, which was more compelling than his priceless art collection.

I stretched my arm out, pointed to the TV and said, "That's what *I* want to do."

BREAK FREE FROM SELF-DOUBT

Being a great interviewer isn't based on your race, gender, height, weight, or looks. The only thing that matters is your ability to create ***compelling*** interviews.

But truth be told, how you feel about yourself *is* important. So if you think you're inadequate in some way, that's something you may want to look into.

When I was young, I had a lazy eye, and it wasn't until my twenties that I had an operation to correct it. Before that operation, I didn't think I was capable of doing television interviews. That may sound silly, but in my mind, it was a real roadblock due to all the teasing I got as a kid. My advice to you is, if you have a personal or physical "roadblock," and it's fixable, correct it. But again, it's only a roadblock if *you believe* it's a roadblock. There are outstanding interviewers of all shapes, sizes, and colors. Looking back, if I didn't get that operation, my lazy eye might have provided me with something unique.

When interviewers ask me if they're tall enough or skinny enough to do this, I always think of Ed Lucas. When Ed was a kid, he was struck by a line drive playing baseball and was blinded. But he loved baseball so much that he'd go to Yankee Stadium and talk to the players, which eventually led to him interviewing Willie Mays, Mickey Mantle, and many of the greatest stars of the game. An award-winning reporter, he's even had a book written about his life called *Seeing Home: The E• Lucas Story*.

What's essential is your ability to *comfort* and *connect* with people and to create *compelling* interviews. Those are the three requirements to become an exceptional interviewer.

A.B.I. - "ALWAYS BE INTERVIEWING"

If you're familiar with the movie *Glengarry Glen Ross,* you've seen the "A.B.C. – Always Be Closing" scene. Well, as an interviewer, you want to "A.B.I. – Always Be Interviewing." As a coach for podcasters and radio/TV interviewers, I'm always surprised by the number of people who ask, "How do I practice interviewing?"

Easy! You practice in life.

For many years, I worked as a hotel concierge, seated at a desk and assisting guests who would ask things like, "What's there to do in town? Where should we go to dinner?" I treated each interaction like an interview. Guests from all over the world suddenly became my real-life talk show guests.

I'd ask,

> "Where are you coming from?"
>
> "What's it like?"
>
> "How is it different from America?"
>
> "What do you do for fun over there?"

Their answers helped me suggest the best things for them, and they liked how curious I was. Listening and allowing people to talk enabled me to learn about their lives.

You can practice interviewing at any job. For example, if you work the counter at McDonald's, you usually have a minimum of one minute with each customer. Ask a few open-ended questions, which cannot be answered by a "yes" or "no." For example, "That's a cool shirt, where did you get it?" You might one day ask that same question to David Dobrik. Asking questions you could conceivably ask a celebrity gives you the best practice. A good manager won't object because they'll see it as excellent customer service. You can do forty quick interviews per shift!

TALK BIG TIP

You can practice interviewing on dates. Ask open-ended questions, listen, and then follow up with good questions. Be present and in the moment. These are the same elements that go into a successful celebrity interview.

Every day of your life should include interviews. A.B.I. – Always Be Interviewing.

"ALWAYS BE INTERVIEWING" BENEFITS

Years ago, I went with my producer on a trip to New York City. We were developing a television talk show but were having difficulty assembling a seasoned production team. One night we went for dinner in Times Square, and as we were eating, I noticed an elderly woman seated next to us, dining alone. I started talking with her and basically interviewed her about her life. It was a lot of fun.

Then she asked us, "What do you do in Los Angeles?"

I explained we were developing a talk show.

She said, "Oh, my daughter is Ellen Brown, the Director of *The Tonight Show with Jay Leno.*"

My jaw hit the floor! Within a week, my producer was in the control booth of *The Tonight Show,* and after explaining our situation, Ellen recommended Liz Plonka, who'd been the Director for years on *Late*

Night with Conan O'Brien. We met with Liz, and along with her technical team, she became our show's Director. Within weeks we were shooting the pilot.

When you're friendly with people and always working on your interviewing skills, you never know who you might meet.

YOUR LIFE 101

Being a good interviewer involves self-examination. Knowing your life inside and out helps you ***connect*** with celebrities.

How many jobs have you had? What were they?

I've worked as a newspaper delivery boy, busboy, stock boy, file clerk, food server, movie usher, bartender, shipping clerk, messenger, bellman, concierge, front desk clerk, real estate broker, personal assistant, pet shop clerk, and more.

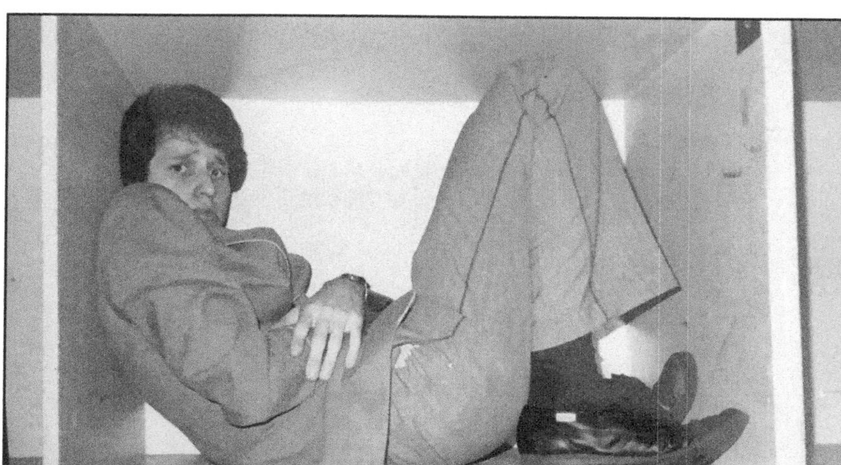

Here I am, stuffed into a luggage bin, while working as a bellman. Celebrities who worked as bellmen include: Tom Hanks, Bradley Cooper, and Tom Cruise.

That's right, I can't hold a job. Believe it or not, most celebrities have had a bunch of "normal" jobs, too. Often while talking with celebrities about their past day jobs, I'm able to empathize with them because *I've been there.* (Although very few of them have worked as a deodorant tester. Hey, it paid the bills!)

In addition to your work history, dig deep and understand your relationships, your successes, failures and setbacks, childhood memories, school memories, and family history.

Having your life experiences readily available, and allowing yourself to share them, increases the likelihood of a celebrity opening up to you. This results in deeper, more ***compelling*** interviews.

Here are some basic questions to start you off. Remember: Your self-knowledge should be extensive.

- ***What's the first thing that you remember in life?***
- ***What was it like growing up in your hometown?***
- ***Describe yourself during your school years.***
- ***What do you most remember about each of your family members?***
- ***What moments have stayed with you from childhood?***
- ***Who was your first friend?***
- ***What conversations with friends do you remember?***
- ***What was your spark or passion as a kid?***
- ***How did you spend your summers?***
- ***What led up to your first kiss?***

- ***What have been the most traumatic events of your life?***
- ***If you created a highlight reel of your life, what would be on it?***

Rather than trying to recollect such moments during a live interview, it's a head start to know them in advance, in vivid detail.

Being open about your life isn't always easy. At the age of twenty-three, I legally changed my name from Michael Schechter to John Kerwin. "John" from John Travolta and "Kerwin" from Lance Kerwin, who starred on a TV show called *James at 15,* the first show I identified with as a little boy. And I guess John Kerwin sounded more original than James Travolta. The number of celebrities who have *also* changed their name is considerable. For years, I was reluctant to reveal this. Now it's a way for me to ***connect*** and build rapport with many stars.

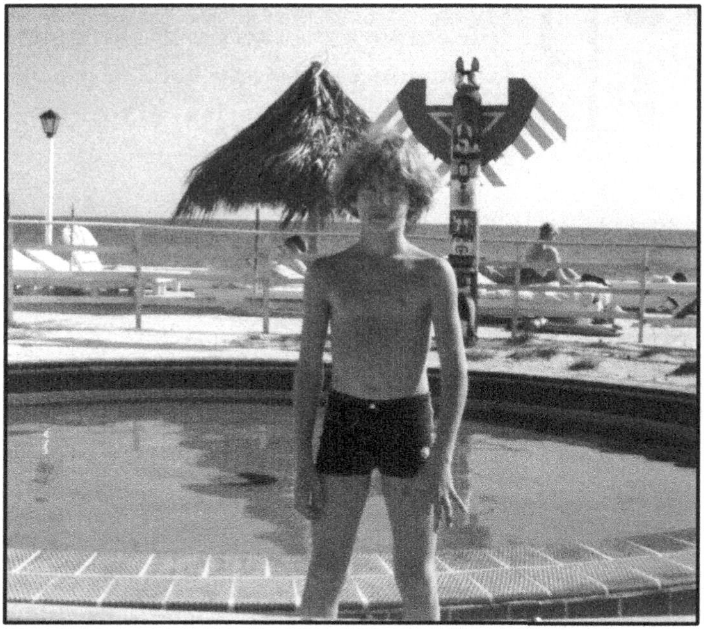

The author previously known as Michael Schechter.

Know your life and decide what you're willing to share. Believe it or not, there was a time when Johnny Carson discussing his divorce on national television was a big deal. Nowadays, interviewers will commiserate with celebrities on their battles with drug abuse, depression, health issues, and many other personal matters. If you really want a celebrity to open up to you, be brave enough to do so yourself.

I've been very moved by personalities such as Whoopi Goldberg mentioning during an interview that she was once homeless, or David Letterman bringing up his quintuple bypass heart surgery. If you're going to create truly ***compelling*** interviews, look deep within your own life and pinpoint the highest of the highs and the lowest of the lows. Sharing those moments will put you on the path of being a great interviewer.

TALK BIG TIP

Knowing your life makes it easier to *connect* with anyone, whether it's a potential client or a first date. Sharing stories from your life encourages others to do the same, and in the process creates a bond between you and those most important to you.

DISCOVERING YOUR UNIQUE PATH

While working for a late-night TV show, I once interviewed a child star, which led to hosting another talk show featuring famous children.

Never in a million years would I have seen that coming! It was a blast interviewing kid stars from Disney and Nickelodeon shows. We had a studio audience packed with 5-11-year-olds. Talk about getting out of my ***comfort*** zone! From the very first day, I had one main objective: Don't look creepy!

Turns out, it was a lot easier than I thought. The trick was getting in touch with my inner child and remembering all the things I cared about as a kid. And, as with all of my interviews, I was super curious about what these teen celebrities were into: Harry Potter, fidget spinners, or the Musical.ly app.

The kicker is that all of a sudden, I was in teen magazines like *Girls' Worl•* and *J-14,* with pictures of me interviewing these kid stars. I remember being so excited, going to the newsstand at five o'clock in the morning and asking the guy, "Did you get the latest issue of *Girls' Worl•*?"

The guy looked at me like he wanted to call 911.

Hosting a kids' show was one of the most wonderful and unexpected surprises of my career thus far, and it started from just one interview.

Here's another example of where this profession can take you. Years ago, when I was working as a standup comedian at New York City's famed Catch a Rising Star comedy club, one of the regulars was Jon Stewart. At the end of the night, he and I sometimes shared taxi rides together. Back then, Jon's act focused on growing up, dating, and being Jewish. He had absolutely zero material about politics.

Cut to a few years later and he's interviewing celebrities on *The Jon Stewart Show* for MTV. Once again, the content was non-political. But as soon as he was picked to host Comedy Central's *The Daily Show,* within a year he became *the* hip authority on politics. It got to the point where people were asking if he was going to run for president!

You don't know where celebrity interviewing will take you—and you should embrace that.

As for what I'm embracing, even though I've interviewed countless celebrities on a number of TV talk shows, my best interviews are yet to come. After I finish writing this book, I'll prepare for my next

You never know where interviewing celebrities might take you. Here I am in the teenzine, J-14, interviewing August Maturo from Disney's TV series *Girl Meets World*. *Photo by Lucie Aleks.*

show. I don't know what it will be or where it will air, I just know I'll be interviewing celebrities in a way no one has ever done before. This might sound crazy, but if I died today my biggest regret would be it happened prior to me hosting the next, best talk show.

IT'S GOOD TO BE THE PRINCE

It's 2011 and people are staring at me. In the street, at the grocery store, everywhere. Finally, at Costco, a guy walks up to me and says, "What are you doing here, Prince William?"

Turns out I looked a lot like the Duke of Cambridge. This was back when he was engaged to Kate Middleton and before he went bald. A nice guy gave me his business card and told me he was a lookalike agent, and that I could make big money with his help. Within weeks I was doing sketches as Prince William on *Ellen* and *The Tonight Show with Jay Leno.*

I was Prince William for a while.
Photo by George Kritikos.

I booked a gig at a polo club for a billionaire's birthday party and rode in on a horse along with a fake Kate Middleton. During that party, I told the guest of honor what I did for a living and convinced him to sit for an interview in front of about 200 guests. That went well and he quickly put me in contact with his friend, which led to my next TV hosting gig.

Always be interviewing.

WHAT'S YOUR REASON?

Why do you want to interview celebrities? Get ready to be asked that question. A lot.

My reason? As far back as I remember, my mother's bedroom always had two chairs facing each other, by her window. Every night for hours, she and I would sit together, and she'd tell me about her life, her problems, her boyfriends, and the events of the day. It was there with my mom where I first learned to interview. She had this test—if at any point she sensed I wasn't paying attention, she'd tell me to repeat her last sentence. If I got it wrong… WHACK! Yet that's how I learned to listen.

I also had to ask good questions. One time she said her current boyfriend was acting angry and she didn't know why.

I asked her, "Does he like strawberry ice cream?"

She shouted, "That's a terrible question! What does strawberry ice cream have to do with what I'm talking about?"

However, when I said, "Do you think he's angry because he just got divorced and, like my dad, he's scared about getting hurt again?"

She'd say, "Aha! *That's* a good question!"

Years later, I was sleeping over at my friend's house, and in the middle of the night I woke up to get a glass of water. I saw my friend's beautiful mother crying in the kitchen.

I asked, "What's wrong?"

She said that she had a fight with her boyfriend.

I said, "Tell me what happened."

We proceeded to sit and talk for over three hours about her relationships. Afterward, she said, "I've never felt so comfortable talking with anyone in my life."

I was *eight*!

Then she said, "If only you were twenty years older, I'd want to date you."

I remember thinking, "Wow, there really *is* something to this interviewing!"

Those nightly interview sessions with my mother, along with having a Sunday Father who always took me to the movies, led to the idea of interviewing celebrities. The icing on the cake was unrestricted access to television, and throughout my childhood I gobbled up thousands of hours of interviews. Other boys had posters of Michael Jordan in their room—I had Johnny Carson! Seriously. It hung right next to my poster of Cheryl Ladd from *Charlie's Angels.*

What's your reason? What has made you become a celebrity interviewer? You *will* be asked.

From my bedroom wall to a television studio. Interviewing my boyhood crush, Cheryl Ladd. *Photo by George Kritikos.*

WHO WOULD YOU INTERVIEW?

Here's another question you'll get: "If you could interview any celebrity, living or dead, who would it be?"

For me, it's Elvis Presley. Why? It's hard to believe, but Elvis never had a great interview. This was probably due to his manager, Colonel Tom Parker, carefully protecting his image.

I've read many books about Elvis and studied his life. He was not only unusually talented, but also very wise and spiritual. Some say his work speaks for itself, but I believe the right interview, at the right time, would have only added to his legacy. Maybe even saved his life!

AN INTERVIEW QUESTION EXERCISE

1. Pick a random celebrity, living or dead.
2. In five minutes or less, write a dozen interview questions.
3. Now research the celebrity.
4. Go back to your questions and see how you can improve them.

If you do this exercise every day for a month, you'll be amazed at the results. You'll be able to create and fine tune questions with ease.

YOUR INTERVIEWS CAN BE IMMORTAL

Every ardent Bruce Lee fan knows the name Pierre Berton. Mr. Berton hosted a Canadian talk show, where he interviewed Lee in 1971. It's the only English-speaking television interview ever done with the martial arts legend. Lee was booked on *The Tonight Show Starring Johnny Carson* but died before that interview took place. Some Bruce Lee fans have watched that black-and-white Pierre Berton interview a hundred times. It's astonishing how your interviews with celebrities can be immortal.

MY FAVORITE CELEBRITY INTERVIEW

Once you start interviewing well-known public figures, "Who's your favorite interview," is another question you'll get. The good news is, your answer will change as you do more and more interviews.

David Carradine, the late star of *Kung Fu* and *Kill Bill,* was my favorite. Aside from being a lifelong fan, when we met there was unusually good chemistry. He also strongly suggested I take up karate.

As a boy I took karate lessons, but there wasn't much money. I remember my mother signing me up for lessons but not being able to pay for the expensive uniform. So, every week, I'd go to karate class wearing my pajamas. There were these tough kids in class wearing uniforms with patches of big fists and swords . . . my uniform had little boats on it. I wasn't dressed for fighting; I was dressed for napping. Anyway, after I reached yellow belt, my mother couldn't afford the lessons anymore and I had to quit.

When my mother died years later, she left a letter explaining how she watched my David Carradine interview and decided to set up a fund so I'd be able to take karate again. She wanted me to finally reach my childhood dream of becoming a black belt.

Black belt ceremony with Grandmaster Kim.

So there I was, the oldest student in my local karate school.

No matter how many injuries I had, or how badly I wanted to quit, I simply couldn't and wouldn't. After years of struggle, I reached the rank of black belt—one of the greatest accomplishments of my life. All thanks to my mother and, in part, David Carradine.

INTERVIEWS ARE NOT COMMERCIALS

The thought of an interview being a commercial for a celebrity's movie, TV show, YouTube channel, or book, is offensive to me. That's like telling a film director that the purpose of their movies is to sell popcorn.

You're the Coppola, the Spielberg, the Scorsese, and the Tarantino of your interviews. You're trying to reveal the human condition, to touch people's lives, and to entertain them. You're doing everything in your power to allow your subject to demonstrate their talent, share their life lessons, and create revealing moments to last forever.

While you also want to aggressively plug their latest projects, I'm adamant in saying, aim higher and **TALK BIG!**

KNOW WHAT YOU WANT

Your vision of what you want must be clear, whether it's to have a successful late-night or daytime talk show, conduct celebrity interviews for a widely viewed podcast, YouTube channel, or talk to stars on the red carpet at the Oscars. Whatever the goal, visualize it in your mind. As you move toward that goal, it may change, and that's fine. But every day, think about exactly what you want, as often as possible.

I was educated in the New York City public school system, which was, no surprise, terrible. I basically got a diploma in survival. In tenth grade, I decided to go to an Ivy League college, specifically Cornell University. This was thought of as impossible in my family, in my school, everywhere except in my mind. Not to mention, my grades and SAT scores were low. Clearly, Ivy was out of my League. I remember being laughed at and surprised at how mean people could be when all I did was express my dream.

I started reading up on anything I could find about Cornell. I had a clear vision that I would go there. Back then, there was no *The Secret* or vision boards, only having an obsessive drive. I thought about what I wanted all the time—morning, noon, and night. I imagined myself strolling along those beautiful 740 acres in Ithaca, NY. Everyone I came into contact with learned about my goal.

When I was a high school junior there was a college fair held in the cafeteria, and Cornell had a representative from their admissions department. His name was Rene Cabrera, and he would serve as my mentor from that point on. As a senior, I listened closely to Rene and worked very hard to improve my SAT scores. I also went to the Cornell University campus for three personal interviews. As unlikely a candidate as I was, one of the people I interviewed with said, "I'm not sure I've ever met anyone who wanted to go to Cornell as much as you do. Even though your grades and scores are subpar, I'm going to give you a favorable recommendation." I wrote him a thank you note with a picture of me on the Arts quad standing next to the statue of Ezra Cornell.

I did everything I could to make my application as strong as possible, including volunteering at Lennox Hill Hospital, and getting involved in every possible high school extracurricular activity. I even played a munchkin in *The Wizar• of Oz.* (I was 6'3".)

Finally, the letter I'd been waiting for arrived in the mail and... I got accepted! It was the most incredible day of my life.

My father told me, "I never thought you'd get in. Now I believe you can do anything."

It was the nicest thing my father had ever said to me.

That journey of getting into Cornell has become a template for everything I've ever wanted to do since. It always seems to be a similar process. I choose a high goal that I really want, people laugh at me and say I can't do it, I work really hard and think about it all the time, then it happens. Even writing this book has been like that. I heard, "You're going to do what?"

I said, "I'm going to write a book about how to interview celebrities, which will inspire people to reach their dreams."

They'd say, "You're wasting your time. It'll never happen."

Well, here we are.

1. Create a clear vision in your mind of what you want.
2. Then let the world know about it, get supporters, and work hard. It will come to you.

My current vision is for this book to be the industry standard on interviewing celebrities.

Beyond that, I'm planning to host a new breakthrough talk show featuring celebrity interviews.

Have a clear vision of what you want, and then become obsessed with getting it.

3 INTERVIEW CATEGORIES

Your style, as an interviewer, will come to you organically through trial and error. In this chapter, we'll discuss different methods of interviewing, but you may also come up with a unique style that's never been done. Or perhaps it will be a hybrid of two or more of the styles listed here.

No particular style is right or wrong. What's important is that your style matches your passion, and that people find it *compelling.*

ONE-ON-ONE

Without a doubt, talking with a guest one-on-one provides the best chance for a landmark interview. There's no studio audience, no band, and no sidekick. With no distractions, it's the purest interview form that exists. In fact, when studying a list of the highest-rated television interviews of all time, unless the interviewees were a couple, they were all done one-on-one.

- **Oprah Winfrey & Michael Jackson (1993)**
- **Barbara Walters & Monica Lewinsky (1999)**
- **David Frost & Richard Nixon (1977)**
- **Steve Kroft & Bill and Hillary Clinton (1992)**
- **Anderson Cooper & Stormy Daniels (2018)**
- **Matt Lauer & Barack Obama (2008)**
- **Diane Sawyer & Whitney Houston (2002)**
- **Barbara Walters & John and Patsy Ramsey (2000)**
- **Bill O'Reilly & Barack Obama (2011)**
- **Diane Sawyer & Caitlyn Jenner (2017)**

Current podcasts such as *WTF with Marc Maron, The Tim Ferriss Show, The Joe Rogan Experience,* and *Armchair Expert with Dax Shepard* are (mostly) versions of this form.

The one-on-one interview may also take place in the celebrity's home. Such was the case when Gayle King interviewed R. Kelly in 2019, and when Martin Bashir spoke with Michael Jackson over the span of eight months, May 2002 to January 2003. The relaxed environment allows the guest to open up more than they might in a sterile television studio environment.

Of course, there are always exceptions. In 2006, Oprah Winfrey interviewed Dave Chappelle in front of a studio audience, and that discussion was very revealing. Because Dave was so accustomed to getting big laughs, the audience's presence didn't dictate the tone of the interview—he did. What made that interview truly ***compelling*** were the parallels between interviewer and interviewee. When Oprah asked a question, it was as if she was asking it to herself. And when Dave answered, he may as well have been answering for Oprah.

Jerry Seinfeld's *Comedians in Cars Getting Coffee* is another example of the one-on-one interview. Jerry talks to a celebrity while driving around in a vintage car, stopping at various locations. This high-quality web series is well-edited and often insightful.

Every now and then, a one-on-one interview becomes historic. Such was the case when Merv Griffin interviewed Christine Jorgensen, the first person in the United States to become widely known for having sex reassignment surgery. Merv's 1970 interview was done with dignity and gave Americans a better understanding of what it meant to be a transsexual. Almost fifty years later, Diane Sawyer interviewed Bruce Jenner in 2015, right before he transitioned to Caitlyn Jenner, and then two years afterward. Once again, a celebrity interview was the vehicle that helped inform and educate the world.

Today, we're privileged to witness great talk show interviewers work in long form. David Letterman's *Our Next Guest Needs No Introduction* allows him to break free from the limitations and time constraints he had on his talk show. Conan O'Brien's podcast, *Conan O'Brien Needs a Friend*, is another stellar example of an extended, one-on-one interview.

The Television Academy (www.emmys.com) has a growing collection of in-depth one-on-one interviews available online. My only issue with them is, the interviewer is always off-camera. I believe the dynamic between interviewer and interviewee is a necessary part of a great interview. That said, they're professionally produced, and I like how the interviewers tell their subject beforehand, "You must think about this interview historically—as if you're looking at this fifty years in the future."

All celebrity interviews should be thought of that way.

THE TV STUDIO AUDIENCE INTERVIEW

The TV studio audience interview is the most exciting and energetic of all formats. The celebrities are not only dressed to look their best, they're also at their most charming, feeding off of the energy from the audience. This is my favorite type of interview. One reason is that the audience lets you know if something is funny, touching, phony, or even offensive. You can hear and feel their responses. After all, you're sharing the interview with them.

During the TV studio audience interview, you always have a good idea of how things are going. The guest is hyperaware of the crowd getting bored, restless, or even angry. If a celebrity shares a personal opinion and hears even one person hiss, that may cause them to clam up and halt any further discussion on that subject. I always think of Tom Cruise being interviewed by Matt Lauer in 2005. It was a one-on-one, heated discussion with Cruise getting about as angry as we've ever seen him in an interview. There's no way that would have ever happened in front of a TV studio audience. When Cruise was on Oprah that same year, from the moment he appeared onstage, the studio audience went wild, screaming for their idol. He came out with almost super-human energy, smiling, entertaining, and even jumping on Oprah's couch. It was the audience driving that energy.

I once did a one-on-one interview with comedian Andy Dick. He was smart, personable, and not at all wacky with me. If the interview had been done in front of a TV studio audience, it would've been a completely different story.

Try doing an interview in front of an audience to find out if that style is right for you.

From the first time I interviewed in front of a live audience, I knew it was for me. Nothing can replicate that experience.

Initially, the TV studio where I worked was too small to hold an audience. So I got a sound effects sampler machine and programmed in various responses, such as big laugh, medium laugh, chuckle, and applause. Then I asked someone to operate the machine while watching the interview live. While this process added laughter and applause throughout the interview, it was a crazy idea. I used to be amused when the guest got upset because "the audience" wasn't "laughing" at their jokes.

My guest and I were craving a real studio audience.

If laughs and entertainment are your goal, then the TV studio audience interview might be your mug of tea. The downside is that it's much more difficult for the celebrity to be revealing when there's a studio audience present. But if, like me, you enjoy escaping from reality without the benefit of controlled substances, then this could be the perfect form for you.

THE GUERILLA INTERVIEW

The people at TMZ have mastered the guerrilla interview, which is an impromptu public meeting. If you're resourceful, you may also score these types of interviews.

Here's something I did when I was starting out and wanted to interview classic TV celebrities. I heard the TV Land Awards® show was taping in Hollywood. They refused to give me a red carpet press pass, so I went to a rug store and bought a 3' x 6' remnant of red carpet. Along with my camera person, I stood across the street from the Hollywood Palladium, where the event took place, and laid down the tiny red carpet. I was wearing a suit and holding a professional-looking hand mic. As recognizable celebrities appeared, I invited them over for an interview. Most liked the idea, and I ended up doing about twenty-five interviews. It was so bananas, some of them talked about it on the *real* red carpet. This led to the producers inviting us inside to watch the show, after which I nabbed another twenty or so interviews.

An infinite number of variations to work the system is possible. I recently saw a video shot from the point of view of a cop's bodycam as he interrogated a criminal. I immediately thought, why didn't I think of that! Wearing one of those would be an inexpensive way to do guerrilla interviews! (Remember: You heard it here first.)

The guerrilla celebrity interview is a low-cost way to not only practice interviewing celebrities, but also to build up your reel to get future work.

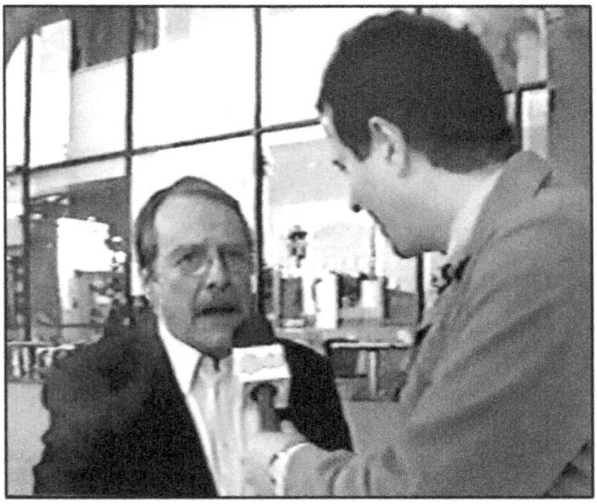

Interviewing funnyman Martin Mull across the street from The TV Land Awards.

THE RED CARPET INTERVIEW

To me, working the red carpet is like doing drive-by interviews. It's a noisy, competitive environment, and you're lucky to get sixty seconds with any given celebrity. Not to mention, you don't have their undivided attention, and the quality of the video/audio is less than ideal. You'll also contend with the celebrity's publicist pushing them to the next interview, and if it's an award show, it's even more chaotic.

However, with stamina and perseverance, you can score some memorable, short interviews with big name stars.

TALK BIG TIP

- **Look professional yet approachable**
- **Prepare quick, simple questions**
- **Do your best to elicit honest answers that'll translate into shareable sound bites on social media and elsewhere**

Aside from questions regarding their part in the event, I've asked uncomplicated questions like, "If not this, what would you be doing tonight?"

And "How does this compare to your very first red carpet event?"

I've also found that working in a plug for them, *within the question,* delivers a longer, better answer.

For example, "In your book *Fame,* you talk about your childhood dream of becoming a Hollywood star. How does this night compare with that dream?"

With a question like that, you're mentioning something important to them, which may elicit a more elaborate answer.

Work a plug (i.e., about their latest work/book, etc.) into your question to get richer, more interesting answers.

Personally, I've never liked red carpet interviews because the surrounding atmosphere is like a Black Friday sale. A frenzy of pushing and yelling and you don't even go home with a bargain Xbox. After doing a few of these, it'll be obvious whether you love 'em or hate 'em.

TALK BIG TIP

Before going to a wedding or a networking event, go through the guest list and peruse the social media pages of the attendees. Jot down things that are important to them, and use those details as ice-breakers when you meet. Think of it as benevolent stalking.

THE AMBUSH INTERVIEW

You must decide whether or not you're on the side of the celebrity. I strongly advise creating positive experiences with people rather than trapping or ambushing them, because very few interviewers are good at it. Documentarian Michael Moore, in films like *Roger & Me, Bowling for Columbine,* and *Fahrenheit 9/11,* has built a lucrative career with the ambush interview.

Early in his career, sportscaster Jim Rome interviewed NFL quarterback Jim Everett. Before they sat down, Rome, who was making a name for himself as a sarcastic wise guy, had been calling Jim Everett, "Chris," insinuating he was female tennis player, Chris Evert.

During their 1994 interview, Everett warned Rome, "If you call me Chris to my face *one more time . . .*"

Rome looked right at him and said, "Chris."

Everett tackled Rome to the floor, and the interview was over.

Wrong as he was, Jim Rome was acting in character. He was the jerk people loved to watch. Even more, the jerk people loved to watch get his butt kicked. And Everett came out looking great as well. Every guy I knew watched that interview at least three times. Who got hurt? Maybe Rome was sore for a day, but his career took off like a rocket. Again, this is not my style, but if you're an "in your face" interviewer, this is yet another example of how you can find success.

Just be warned, this style is risky. Mel Gibson was interviewed many years after he apologized to virtually everyone for inappropriate things he'd said. When he had a new movie coming out, he was being interviewed, and at first, the interviewer was very friendly and asked pertinent questions. It wasn't until the end of the interview when he brought up Gibson's past comments. Gibson got angry and defensive, and the interview ended on a very sour note.

I refuse to ambush celebrities. A long time ago I interviewed a star who had a drinking problem. After discussing the highlights of his career, I asked if he considered himself an alcoholic.

His expression said, "I want to kill you."

But instead, he said, "I explained to your producer that I didn't want to discuss that area of my life. Why would you do that?"

I answered with dumb logic, "Don't you feel the public has a right to know?"

"No," he snapped, and walked off the set.

I felt terrible and vowed never to do that again.

If you're interested in investigative journalism, watch Mike Wallace in the 2019 documentary, *Mike Wallace is Here.* Becoming a muckraker, as he refers to himself, is something he discovered worked well for him. "I found my bliss" is how he put it.

It reminds me of the time, early in Phil Donahue's career, when a guest cancelled and, to fill time, he went into the studio audience with a microphone to ask people questions. When that worked, Phil said the moment was "nirvana" as it provided him with a unique approach.

The key is that each of those styles worked perfectly for that particular interviewer. Finding one's style comes through trial and error, and hitting upon it is something of a mystery because it's a meshing of your personality, talent, temperament, and other intangibles, and most notably how audiences receive you in that style. As with the stand-up comedian searching for their "hook," it usually evolves over time. I want you to find the style that works best for you.

THE GOSSIP INTERVIEW

TV personalities Andy Cohen, Wendy Williams, and the late Joan Rivers have been experts at the gossip interview, which rewards a nervy, chatty personality. If your guilty pleasures include supermarket tabloids and blind item websites, and you don't mind being whacked by a Hermes® bag, then this might be the area for you.

My opinion is you're naturally at odds with celebrities when the goal is dredging up scandalous rumors about their lives. However, we're living in a time where gossip is the driving force behind reality shows and acts as the foundation of many a celebrity's career. Not to mention this style has been around forever, going as far back as 1930s newspaper columnist Walter Winchell.

That said, the gossip interview can be very enlightening. Check out the RuPaul podcast *What's the Tee?* with Michelle Visage. In one episode, RuPaul interviews *Will & Grace* star Sean Hayes, who discusses being gay more openly than I've seen with any other interviewer. Ru naturally creates an all-inclusive environment, effortlessly gossiping about sex and other "taboo" subjects. There's an honesty to this podcast that comes off as genuine. (By the way, *What's the Tee?* means "What's the truth?")

So if the gossip interview fits your personality, and you have good medical coverage, a built-in audience is waiting for you.

THE GHOST INTERVIEW

During my career, I've sometimes spent hours interviewing a celebrity in person, and other times we weren't even in the same country. Masterful interviewer Terry Gross hosts *Fresh Air,* a National Public Radio show out of Philadelphia, and rarely meets her guests—the interviews are done via satellite or over the phone. I call this *ghost interviewing* because you never actually meet the celebrity. It's common with many podcasts and talk radio shows.

Sometimes with Q&A print interviews, you don't even talk with the celebrity, but rather email their publicist a list of questions. Then a few days later, the publicist sends back the answers. I've had to get written guarantees that the celebrity was, in fact, the one answering my questions.

TALK BIG TIP

If you're not interviewing the celebrity face-to-face, make sure you have a confirmation from their publicist that the answers to your questions are coming directly from the celebrity.

When starting out, I urge that you only do in-person interviews. Otherwise you're not fully experiencing key elements such as rapport, spontaneity, body language, eye contact, and even something as simple as a handshake or a hug. It will build up your confidence having met even a local celebrity face-to-face. You'll take pictures together, and unlike ghost interviewing, you'll have proof that you interviewed your celebrity in the flesh.

THE PRINT INTERVIEW

If descriptive writing is one of your passions, the print interview offers you opportunities not found in any other medium. I've written celebrity profiles for magazines which are a combination of editorial passages along with transcribed portions of the interview. Writing for print may include describing where and when the interview took place, the initial meeting of the celebrity, their outfit, mood, etc. It's almost like a behind-the-scenes expose intertwined with an interview. You'll also be "setting up" certain parts of the interview with descriptive writing.

For example, "After taking a spontaneous nude dip in her swimming pool, Lana donned a Japanese silk robe and returned to our table to talk about the pressures of being a sex symbol."

The best print interviewers write in such a way that they literally transport you to the interview—whether it's on a film set, an exotic island, or in a Beverly Hills mansion. It's as if you're reading the work of an interviewer/novelist.

When I was in college, I was obsessed with the *Playboy* magazine interviews. That's right, the interviews! These are readily available online and compiled in book form. I also recommend reading classic *Rolling Stone* magazine interviews. You can find many of them online, too. Lawrence Grobel, author of *The Art of The Interview,* is one of my favorite interviewers of celebrities. If print becomes your area of concentration, I recommend reading his book.

Beyond that, check out Richard Merryman's interview with Marilyn Monroe in the August 1962 edition of *Life Magazine.*

THE BOOK INTERVIEW

Filmmaker/comedian Judd Apatow's 2015 book *Sick in the Hea•* is comprised of interviews he did with comics, from when he was a teenager up to the 2010's. Some of the funny people he spoke with include Adam Sandler, Amy Schumer, Jim Carrey, Sarah Silverman, and Louis C.K. Did he have any idea that one day those early interviews would be turned into a best-selling book? Of course not. But you never know what the lifespan of your interviews will be. More important, you never know where the careers of celebrities you interview will go.

Some years ago, I was fortunate to interview the maverick film director Henry Jaglom. During our conversation, Jaglom mentioned he was friends with legendary film director Orson Welles and that he recorded their conversations. Later those conversations were transcribed into a book called *My Lunches with Orson.* Henry and Orson had great rapport, which translated into a series of enlightening interviews due to their ***comfort*** level, strong ***connection***, and ***compelling*** conversations.

Some interviews disappear and then reemerge with new life years or decades later. I can't tell you how many interviews I've watched or read where the interviewer and subject had both passed away. As I've said, your interviews can be eternal.

The book interview is a format that will likely come to you after a long career. However, there are exceptions. If you're friends with a star like

Interviewing the maverick film director, Henry Jaglom. *Photo by George Kritikos.*

Kanye West and he agrees to let you interview him, and you're wise enough to tape it, then you, too, may become an author.

TALK BIG TIP

Keep a file of every interview (both edited and unedited), pre-interview questions, tape recordings, and pictures. The life of your interviews may be full of surprises and unexpected value.

THE PARODY INTERVIEW

The parody interview is a fake conversation that satirizes the celebrity and/or the interviewer. Examples of this are comedic actor Martin Short's Jiminy Glick, Sasha Baron Cohen's many outlandish characters (Ali G, Borat, Bruno), *The Eric An●re Show* on Adult Swim, and Zach Galifianakis's Funny or Die show *Between Two Ferns.*

The two basic types of parody interviews are:

1. Where the celebrity is in on the joke (Jiminy Glick, Eric Andre, *Between Two Ferns*)

2. The celebrity is ambushed (Ali G, Borat, Bruno)

The latter can sometimes be dangerous and may lead to possible arrest. But when done properly, the pay-off can be worth the risk.

The "celebrity approved" parody can be inventive and imaginative. Usually the interview is prearranged, and the celebrity is prepared for the insults. Sometimes the producers provide scripted insults to fire back and the interview becomes a back-and-forth roast. Usually this sort of interview is done by someone experienced with traditional interviewing.

My problem with this form is that it's not really an interview. It's a sketch. That said, it can be very funny and successful. Barack Obama's *Between Two Ferns* appearance has over thirty million views.

An interesting variation on this theme is the celebrity giving a fake interview to a real interviewer. The late, great Andy Kaufman used to do this. You never knew what was real or made up. Fortunately, an interviewer named Tom Cottle, who had a background in psychology, somehow got Andy to give a straight interview and it became an instant classic. I believe it was the only extended, real interview Andy ever gave.

THE TAGALONG INTERVIEW

If a celebrity wants their friend/child/lover to be a part of the interview, agree to it. I once landed an interview with actor Ed Begley Jr. on the condition that Scott Harris, who built Ed's revolutionary "green" house, also be included. It worked out well because Scott happened to be a fine guest. The way to handle this situation is:

- Show respect by asking questions to the tagalong guest first
- Explore the relationship between the two of them
- When you sense the main guest/celebrity is satisfied, turn the focus of the interview onto them, which should comprise about 80 percent of the entire interview

TALK BIG TIP

If your interview is televised, make sure the main celebrity guest is seated closest to you. This psychologically ensures that the majority of the focus is on them. Also, placing the main celebrity next to you works better for photos.

On her podcast, *Anna Farris Is Unqualified*, Anna interviewed Jimmy Kimmel and his wife Molly McNearney in 2018. Anna did a great job involving Molly during a bit called "Sexual Deal Breakers." For instance, would it be a Deal Breaker if one spouse wanted a "Hall Pass?" It was a fun way to organically bring Molly into the conversation, while observing Jimmy in a way you wouldn't as host of his own show. Anna, with her sexy comic persona, created a fun and non-threatening exchange.

The bottom line is, if a star wants to do an interview along with his spouse, his friend or his dog's acupuncturist, say "Yes!" If an influencer wants to discuss her spiritual awakening and bring her lifestyle coach, say "No problem!" The more the merrier.

Interviewing actor and environmental activist Ed Begley, Jr., and "green contractor" Scott Harris. *Photo by Lucie Aleks.*

DON'T PIGEONHOLE YOURSELF

While I consider myself primarily a talk show host who interviews celebrities, I've also done one-on-one interviews, on-location interviews, red carpet, print, panel, and podcast interviews. You never know what path your career will take, and you should always be open to different platforms. You may wind up interviewing famous athletes, or you may find yourself writing for a music magazine doing backstage interviews with rock stars. As long as you're professional and maintain a reputation as a trusted confidant, the possibilities are endless. Why?

Because many times, an entire career will come down to one celebrity liking you enough to give you an interview.

That can lead to them recommending you to their colleagues. For example, if you interview television chef Rachael Ray, and she likes you, that interview can lead to you interviewing Wolfgang Puck, Jamie Oliver, Gordon Ramsay, and other celebrity chefs. These types of personalities could become your niche, even if you've never cooked anything more than SpaghettiOs®.

Be open to what comes your way. That unpredictability is part of what makes doing this so much fun.

4 GETTING THE INTERVIEW

The best way to start your career as a celebrity interviewer is seeking out local celebrities; maybe someone who was featured in your hometown newspaper. If the neighborhood dry cleaner has autographed photos on the wall, write down those names, find out what they've done, and if it interests you, ask for an interview. That's the old school way. You can also search for influencers or micro-influencers in your area. Local publications often showcase these people. Remember: every medium needs content, so offering free profiles to local newspapers, magazines, or online publications is a great way to break in. You can also create your own publication or online forum, then contact the local reps for people in your town you'd like to interview. Many times, at that level, you can reach the person directly. Be professional and introduce yourself by saying, "Hi, my name is Jane Smith and I'm an interviewer for the *Spring Valley Ezine.* I've watched your popular vlogs where you sing opera in laundromats and I'd love to share your story with our readers. May I take you to lunch?"

It's that easy. Never underestimate the power of a free lunch.

While not a "local" celebrity, I remember interviewing Drew Barrymore's stand-in when I first started out. She looked a lot like Drew, obviously, and had a great personality. I asked basic questions like, "What exactly does a stand-in do?" and "How did you get into this type of work?" I also asked what interactions she had with the real Drew Barrymore. It was a lot of fun and surprisingly informative.

And whatever you do, no matter the stage of your career, don't be a snob. Interview everyone! After I had some real-world experience, I thought it would be interesting to meet actors who had small roles in some of my favorite films. One of my favorite movies is *Pulp Fiction,* and I thought, what if I interviewed "The Gimp," who was played by an actor named Stephen Hibbert? Or Stuart Rudin, who acted as Miggs, the prisoner in the cell next to Hannibal Lecter in *Silence of the Lambs?* Find creative and satisfying ways to interview people and watch your skills improve.

TALK BIG TIP

Once you've interviewed your first established name, use that interview to get more work.

My first celebrity interview was with Richard Kline, who played Larry Dallas on the '70s TV show *Three's Company.* Within a week, I had a dozen other celebrities lined up. How? Because a video of that interview served as a calling card I sent out to a boatload of publicists.

Start modestly and you'll be surprised how quickly you move up the interviewing ladder.

My first official TV celebrity interview was with Richard Kline, who played Larry Dallas on *Three's Company*. *Photo by Stacy Altman.*

HOW TO CONTACT CELEBRITIES

Based on my experience, I recommend using the website IMDbPro (www.imdb.com). There's an annual subscription fee, but considering the time and energy you'll save, it's totally worth it. I've booked many celebrities thanks to information found through this site. You simply look up a name and up pops their contact info, including publicist, manager, and occasionally, a direct contact. IMDbPro sometimes promotes a free trial period, so you can see for yourself how it works. Whenever you can get anything in Hollywood for free, grab it. Keep in mind, the more "in demand" the star, the more gatekeepers you'll encounter—so don't expect to find Shawn Mendes's cell number. But you'll have a way to reach his people.

PUBLICISTS

A publicist is someone paid to get people publicity. Hence the name. Clever, huh? This is why a publicist is the person most open to your interview request—it's their job to make their clients look favorable in the public eye.

Agents and managers, on the other hand, look to get paid work, and a commission. As an interviewer, you'll mostly be dealing with publicists, and the challenge is demonstrating your request is worth their time. The savvy publicist understands that what you're offering must be the right kind of publicity. Therefore, having highly professional materials is essential. **The publicist may forward your letter, website link, and examples of your work directly to the client. Based on those materials, the celebrity will say yes or no.**

Building good relationships with publicists is critical to gaining access to celebrities.

AUTOGRAPH SHOWS

When you're starting out, you've got to be creative in accessing celebrities. In addition to my faux red carpet, here's another way I was able to get to celebrities. Throughout the year, there are autograph shows in most large cities. They're a low-pressure way for public figures to meet their fans while making money. Usually, each celebrity will rent a small area in a convention center or hotel ballroom. They'll typically display merchandise to sell: autographed pictures, CDs, posters, books—you name it. For a fee, you can take a picture with them. Think of it as a room chockful of celebrities waiting to meet you.

When I was new to the business, I'd go to these shows and meet fifty to a hundred celebrities in one day. I'd prepare interview questions beforehand for all the celebrities who were scheduled to appear. For just a relatively small entry fee, I'd get to practice interviewing celebrities, which helped build my confidence. Many of them would actually say, "You should be a professional interviewer!"

Later, when it's time for your first real celebrity interview, you'll think, "Shoot, if I can interview a hundred people in a noisy convention hall, I can do this!"

But I didn't stop there. Another thing I did, months later, was book guests directly from the autograph shows. After establishing rapport, I'd mention that I had a local talk show and invite them to promote their latest project. I carried business cards, and often left a show with four or five guests booked.

Keep in mind that many celebrities fly in for these events, while others may live in town. I'd concentrate on the ones who lived in my region, Los Angeles, because the others would likely not be available.

TALK BIG TIP

Make friends with one of the staff members before the event. Ask them what time of day the hall or room is the quietest. This way you can have more quality time with each celebrity.

You can also cut to the chase and simply interview the celebrities right there at the event. The primary problem with that idea is that it's very noisy and the celebrity is really there to sell, not be interviewed. Keep in mind, without prior consent you might get pushback if you try taping or filming an interview. I never did this because the environment was usually too noisy—it's actually worse than a red-carpet interview. But if you're persuasive and inventive, you might be able to lure a celebrity away from the main ballroom for an interview.

Many times, I was the first one there in order to get the celebrities at their freshest. Other times, I stayed until the bitter end when they were relaxed (and sometimes drunk), and open to chatting.

If you're respectful and well-prepared, attending autograph shows is a great way to meet and book celebrities.

I first met one of my favorite actors, Eric Roberts, at an autograph convention.
Photo by George Kritikos.

LETTERS, EMAILS, AND DIRECT MESSAGES

Through writing letters, emails, and direct messages, I've reached people you'd think were unreachable. I've also booked countless celebrity interviews this way. It sounds simple, but there's an art to letter writing, and what you learn in this section can bring you into direct contact with the most powerful and influential people in the world.

When I was in my early 20s, I worked as a bellman at a hotel in New York City. It was rough, as my supervisor bossed me around and constantly picked on me. It got so bad I complained to HR, which went nowhere. Rather than punch my supervisor in the nose, I wrote a letter to the owner of the hotel. I even went to a secretarial service (yes, this was a real thing) and paid them to type it and fix any grammatical errors. A few days later the owner, Donald Trump, marched into the hotel with a small entourage. With my letter in hand, he raised hell with senior management. After that, no one bothered me again. That's when I first realized the power of letter writing.

In 2019, I received the following email.

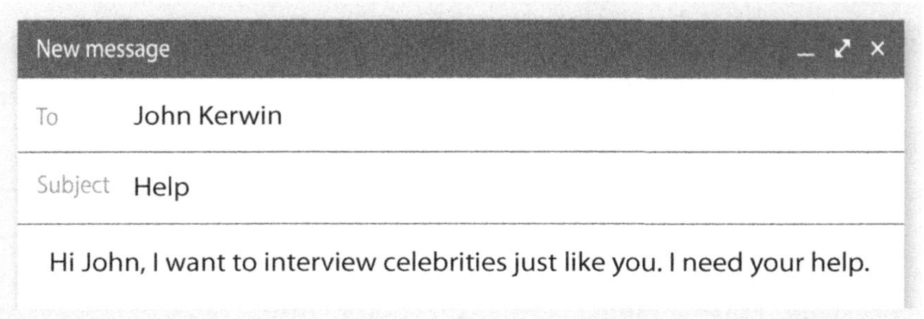

My first reaction was, "Who is this? Why should I help them?"

Now here's an email I received from a different person:

New message

To John Kerwin

Subject Thank you for The John Kerwin Kids' Show

Dear Mr. Kerwin,

Even though my mom is emailing you this, I wrote it all by myself.

I am twelve years old and saw you interview Lizzy Greene on TV. It was awesome. She is my favorite star. I love her on "Nicky, Ricky, Dicky, and Dawn." In fact, I've never missed it once. I thought it was so funny how she taught you yoga and how you played Chubby Bunny with her and how she could barely talk with all the marshmallows in her mouth. I never knew she liked to paint. I also paint. Her story about being clumsy reminded me of how clumsy I am in school.

After I watched it, I told my mom that I want to do what you do and talk to stars on television. Would you please let me know how I can start doing that at my age? I'm a very good student and am like an expert on all Nickelodeon shows. Your help would really mean a lot to me, and I promise to help others in the future if they ask.

Thank you so much for even reading this email.

Sadie

My feeling about this email was very different. I outlined to her mother different ways her daughter could start interviewing and how she could help. I let her mom know she could write back if she had more questions and to update me on how Sadie was doing.

For Sadie, I also emailed some exclusive behind-the-scenes pics of Lizzy Greene.

Let's see why I reacted favorably to the second email. There are eight components to an effective letter, email, or DM.

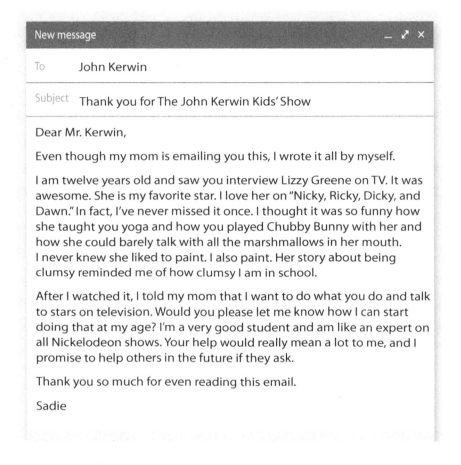

My interview with the talented Lizzy Greene, which was featured in Girls' World magazine. *Photo by Lucie Aleks.*

1. A CLEAR REQUEST

In the first email, his request is not clear. How does he want my help? Does he want interviewing tips? Does he want me to call someone to help him get a job? Does he want me to look over one of his interviews? The request is vague. In fact, I have more questions for him than for most of my celebrity interviews.

In the second email, the request is clear. Sadie is twelve years old and wants to know how to take the first step to interviewing celebrities. *That* I can answer.

2. DEMONSTRATE WHY THEY SHOULD HELP YOU

In the first email there's no reason I feel compelled to help.

In the second email, Sadie mentions that she's a good student and is an expert on Nickelodeon shows. I also sense her sincere passion for this. She creates an argument for me to help her.

3. GIVE SOMETHING BEFORE ASKING

In the first email, I'm given nothing.

In the second email, Sadie says how much she enjoyed my interview with Lizzy Greene. She gives specific examples from the interview. She compliments me by saying the interview was awesome. It makes me feel that she's genuine in her request.

4. USE TACT

The first email is abrupt, disrespectful, and looks like it took ten seconds to compose.

The second email is well thought-out and is also phrased in a sincere, straightforward manner that makes me *want* to help her.

5. DON'T DEMAND OR BEG

The first email sounds like a demand. "I need your help" sounds like I'm required to do something for this guy, like I *owe* him this.

The second email doesn't demand or beg. She just plainly asks.

6. SHOW RESPECT

The second email opens with "Dear Mr. Kerwin" rather than "Hi John." Now, I happen to like being called by my first name, but neither of them knew that. It's proper etiquette to show respect when asking for a favor from someone you don't know. Sadie also thanks me for "even reading this email."

The first email doesn't show any gratitude at all.

7. BE PERSISTENT

Although not relevant in either of these emails, it often takes multiple letters before you finally receive an answer. It once took writing 114 letters before finally getting an interview with a celebrity I admired. That may sound crazy, but it was absolutely worth it. It took a total of forty hours to write those letters, which finally led to an interview with the famous astronomer, Carl Sagan. He even jokingly said to me, quoting his own line, "You've written to me billions and billions of times."

Being persistent in your letter writing is often the difference between success and failure.

TALK BIG TIP

As you perfect your letter writing, your potential to *connect* to anyone in the world is limitless.

8. TEAM EFFORT

The first email comes across as a self-centered demand.

In the second email, Sadie writes, "Your help would really mean a lot to me and I promise to help others in the future if they ask." This leads me to believe that my help will have real meaning in her life, and by helping her, she, in turn, may help other kids. Suddenly the request is a team effort, and that's difficult to say no to.

MY EMAIL TO MARC SUMMERS

When I was interviewing kid celebrities, I wanted to meet Marc Summers, who was the top hosting guy at Nickelodeon® when I was growing up. He hosted the show *Double Dare* and he just seemed to be everywhere. How did I meet and talk with him? You guessed it! I wrote him a letter. He not only responded, but we had lunch together at *Nate 'n Al's,* the one-time legendary deli in Beverly Hills. He's a terrific guy, and he answered all my questions. Because I believe that letter writing is so important, I'll share with you the email I sent him. You'll notice I was very respectful of his career and made a pretty good case on why he should meet with me.

New message

To Marc@MarcSummers.com

Subject From John Kerwin, Host of The John Kerwin Kids' Show

Dear Mr. Summers,

It's always been clear to me how talented you are. It goes beyond doing comedy, magic, etc. You connect incredibly well with people. It's a gift, and I completely recognize and admire it.

I host a children's television show called *"The John Kerwin Kids' Show."* It is a kids' talk show where we have a studio audience and I also interview kid celebrities starring on shows from Nickelodeon and other networks. Guests we've had on include Addison Riecke and Maya Le Clark from *"The Thundermans,"* Sean Ryan Fox from *"Henry Danger,"* and Jade Pettyjohn from *"School of Rock."* Riele Downs from *"Henry Danger"* will be on our next episode. The show has been called *"The Tonight Show for Kids."* We are in this month's *J-14* Magazine (see attached) – they call us "This summer's must-watch show!" In addition to celebrity kids, each show also features a child who has done something extraordinary in the world to help other kids or to help improve our planet. We've taped only six episodes, and the show currently airs on DirecTV®. The shows are shot in HD, and along with my partner, I have complete ownership of them.

Our show already has a management team; however, they tell me that Nickelodeon does all of its original programming in-house and we should look at other platforms. But I believe Nickelodeon may well be the right network for our show.

If you could give me a few minutes of your time, I certainly would appreciate it.

Thank you for your consideration,

John Kerwin

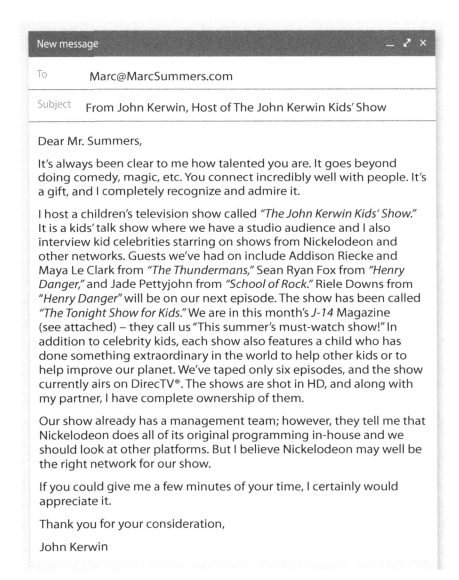

To date, my kids' show hasn't made it to Nickelodeon. But Marc helped in a variety of ways and I gave it my best shot. I co-created what many considered to be the best kids' interview show on television, and I did it for a full year.

People told me there's no way Marc Summers would meet with me, but we met after he read that single email.

While hosting that show, I noticed many children in the studio audience were carrying books from the *Diary of a Wimpy Kid* series. I quickly found out that the author, Jeff Kinney, is the No. 1 children's author in America and chief architect of the $500 million-dollar *Diary of a Wimpy Kid* franchise.

I started reading the books and enjoyed them so much that I wrote a letter to Mr. Kinney. His assistant set up a phone meeting and we talked for over an hour. He gave me tremendous advice and couldn't have been kinder. He even said that when he visited Los Angeles, he wanted me to interview him. Once again, this all came from one letter.

Perfecting your letter writing can put you in touch with anybody. I mean *anybody.*

TALK BIG TIP

Taking the time to write effective letters and messages will help you in all areas of your life. Even the act of writing thought-out thank you letters will have a strong effect on customers, bosses, doctors, and anyone else who's important to you.

HAMMERIN' HANK AARON

Like many young boys, when I was twelve years old I wanted to meet my favorite baseball players. Aside from the pre-game autographs, which were a mob scene, I had to figure out how to meet them in a less chaotic environment. Every day, I'd scour the city newspaper for which I was a delivery boy, and I found out that to make extra money, some players visited new car dealerships and banks to sign autographs. So one day, I called this local bank again and again, until finally someone gave me inside information on the best way to meet Hall of Famer, Hank Aaron.

When the day arrived, I walked into the bank an hour before the autograph session started. I looked around the empty lobby, and sitting alone at a desk in the corner was the legendary home run king. I couldn't believe it! I walked over and talked with him one-on-one about baseball for about thirty minutes, peppering him with a ton of questions I'd prepared. As I finished, a mob of fans entered the bank, starting a line that went all the way around the block. I left the bank feeling like I'd conquered the world!

Making that happen at twelve years old took planning and persistence—the same strategy needed to land a celebrity interview.

- Find out all about the subject (Retired at the time, Hank Aaron already had books written about him; I read two of them)
- Prepare good questions
- Figure out where you can meet them for an interview
- Get intel on the best time to approach them

- Show respect (I made sure to walk into the bank wearing my Hank Aaron baseball jersey)
- Have the guts to follow through
- When approaching, be upbeat, confident, and professional

BROADWAY INTERVIEWS

While still in high school, I'd walk around the NYC theater district at night desperately wanting to see Broadway shows I couldn't afford. One night I noticed a crowd of people outside a theater during intermission. As they filed back into the theater for the second half of the show, the ushers weren't checking for ticket stubs. I thought, "I bet I could get in." So I started sneaking in and seeing the second half of every show on Broadway. If that wasn't enough of a hustle, I'd wait by the stage doors after the show and pretend I was a reporter for my school newspaper, which created many interviewing opportunities with Broadway stars. Sometimes I'd ask them if I could see the show again, in order to complete my "front-page story about them" (It's a miracle my nose didn't start growing.)

Anyway, that's how I got to see the *first* half of the shows. By the time I was seventeen, I'd seen every show and interviewed over a hundred Broadway stars.

You may not be comfortable bending the rules as I did, but the number of creative ways to interview celebrities is infinite. And by the way, when I have to, I still bend the rules.

ROCKY HORROR INTERVIEWS

While my Broadway game was killing it, I was very shy and not doing well with the girls. One day at lunch, sitting at the next table were the two coolest girls in school. I overheard them talking about seeing *The Rocky Horror Picture Show* at the famed 8th Street Playhouse in Manhattan. I'd never heard of it, but I figured if those two were there, it was the place for me.

The following Saturday I went by myself, and it seemed like every awesome teenager in the city was there: straight kids, gay kids, stoners, outcasts, and the prettiest girls I'd ever seen. The problem was I didn't know how to mingle or do anything other than just watch the movie and dream about Susan Sarandon.

The next week, I hatched a plan. I borrowed my father's tape recorder and camera and went back to the theater on Saturday night wearing a white shirt, black tie, and my coolest jeans. I started talking with people in line, saying that I wrote for my school newspaper and was doing a front-page story on *Rocky Horror,* and asked if I could interview them. They practically screamed, "Yes!" I interviewed the flamboyant kids, the OG cosplay ones dressed like Frank-N-Furter, Riff Raff, Magenta . . . everyone. Those kids presented themselves like little celebrities, and they all wanted to be interviewed by me. I was like the kid in Cameron Crowe's movie *Almost Famous,* except instead of writing for *Rolling Stone,* I wrote for...well... nothing.

During one interview, I asked this group of decked out kids, "What do you guys do *after* the movie?"

They said, "We have epic parties."

I said, "Oh . . . you know for my article . . . I really should experience that."

They said, "Of course! You're invited."

At the party, a pretty girl walked up to me and said, "You're the reporter, right?"

"Yes," I said.

"You know what? I think you're full of it."

"You're right, I am."

"That's okay, I still like you."

That's how I met my first girlfriend. I was embodying the most important message in *Rocky Horror*: "Don't Dream It, Be It."

EVEN GARBO GOT INTERVIEWED

In early 2020, I interviewed Edward Lozzi, who once did the impossible—he interviewed Greta Garbo. Along with *The Catcher in the Rye* author J.D. Salinger, at one time Greta Garbo was the most unattainable celebrity interview in the world. A movie star during the 1920s and 30s, she quit show business at the age of 35 and became a recluse, famously saying, "I want to be left alone." She hadn't given an interview since the 1940s.

One day, Edward Lozzi's aunt introduced him to one of her girlfriends, who took a liking to him. Turns out, that woman was lifelong friends with Greta Garbo. The next time a Garbo visit was planned, Edward was told he'd be introduced to her.

Seeing this as the opportunity of a lifetime, Edward read everything he could on Garbo and compiled a long list of questions to store in his head. He wore all white for the meeting, because as he explained,

"I was dressed to meet royalty." The woman laid the ground rules for meeting Garbo: no cameras, no recorders, and only speak when first spoken to.

Behind her dark sunglasses, Garbo sized up Edward, as her friend said complimentary things about him. Slowly, he gained her trust, and soon, Garbo was talking.

When the moment felt right, Edward boldly posed the most important question he'd ever ask: "May I talk with you about your life and career for all the fans who love and care about you?"

Miraculously, she agreed.

Garbo talked about Hollywood being her biggest regret and how "there was no one to share her success with." When Edward followed up by listing off the famous men in her life, she explained that those relationships were publicity stunts and that her only real crush was on James Mason. Edward got wonderful quotes such as, "All I do in life is drift."

She also discussed the day-to-day minutia of her world, like her love for music videos, her addiction to licorice, and how she went incognito to garage sales.

As Edward jokingly told me, "Somehow I managed to do that without reading your book!"

Using Mr. Lozzi's example, through persistence and ingenuity, you can interview any celebrity in the world.

Edward did all the things I advise in this book. He implemented the ***Three C's*.**

Comfort

He made Garbo ***comfortable*** *by showing respect and dressing impeccably. He also made sure her friend of fifty years explained that he was a quality person.*

Connect

He ***connected*** *with her by being conversational, personable, and knowledgeable about her life and career.*

Compel

The interview was ***compelling*** *because it was unprecedented. His questions, and follow-up questions, were worthy of her answers.*

SNOWBALL EFFECT

Once you start interviewing celebrities, getting more bookings becomes easier. The reason is simple—when you do good interviews, celebrities tell each other. When you treat publicists with respect, they want their other clients interviewed by you as well. A good experience for them is a good experience for their clients. It's a snowball effect. You'll wake up one morning and find out a dream celebrity wants you to interview them.

A TV actor will talk about the interview with their fellow cast mates. If they had a good time, the other stars on that show will also want you to interview them. I once interviewed Jillian Shea Spaeder, one of the stars of Disney®'s *Walk the Prank*. She spread the word, and I ended up interviewing the entire main cast. From *Dancing with the Stars*, I've interviewed the host, Tom Bergeron, dancers Anna Trebunskaya, Corky Ballas, and Sharna Burgess, and several celebrities who've appeared on the show.

Word gets around.

5 PREPARATION

Some interviewers, like Barbara Walters, prepare down to the very last detail. Others, like Larry King and Craig Ferguson, barely prepare at all. When starting out, I highly recommend that you fully prepare. You'll be glad you did.

For my first interview with Richard Kline, I studied everything I could get my hands on. I knew his background, education, family life, theater work, and TV and film appearances. I read interviews and even went to the Museum of Television and Radio in Beverly Hills to find obscure clips of his work—anything and everything I could find. I had so much material going into that interview that we could've talked for six hours. As it turns out, he was hilarious and most of my prep wasn't even needed. But it was vital that I had done the work. **That preparation allowed me to be *in the moment* and confident.**

HOW SHOULD YOU DRESS

Avoid suspenders. Unless you're Larry King. Seriously, this is one of the most common questions I get asked. You should wear what feels right for you. I like a suit and tie because it shows that the interview is important to me, and it puts me in a frame of mind to get down to business. When I interviewed kid celebrities, I wore sport jackets that were orange, yellow, and other bright colors along with jeans and Chuck Taylors; that made me feel comfortable and ready for anything, including green slime. Someone like Joe Rogan wears graphic T-shirts, which works well for him on his podcast. Throughout his career, David Letterman wore a sports jacket, shirt, tie, and then chinos and loafers. That style worked for him as a contrast to the impeccable suits and shoes worn by Johnny Carson.

It may sound obvious, but how people and characters dress for television is important. For example, the creators of *Seinfeld* decided that Jerry would always wear solid-colored shirts because his character is "solid." George, on the other hand, would wear plaid shirts, as his character was more chaotic.

Someone like Wolf Blitzer would look ridiculous in a black leather jacket, but for Howard Stern, it's perfect. Experiment to find what feels right for you.

I believe it serves you to dress clean, no matter what your style. It's difficult to command respect if your clothes are wrinkled or dirty. Even Jerry Springer wears a nice jacket.

SHOW ME THE TALENT!

It's a thrill for audiences to witness what made your celebrity famous; the more unique the skill, the better. Find ways to inject their talent into the interview.

Edson Arantes do Nascimento was once the world's greatest soccer player. What he could do with a soccer ball was breathtaking. It was more art than sport. Better known as Pele, each time he was introduced for an interview he entered kicking a soccer ball. He knew that's what people wanted to see. As interesting as his life stories were, at some point during the interview, it was time to grab the soccer ball and show off his skills—and he got roars.

Whether as Lou Grant on *The Mary Tyler Moore Show* or the old man in the Disney/Pixar® film, *UP*, Ed Asner has always been one of America's great comedic actors. During our interview, I did a scene with him to show off his incredible timing and acting. It was thrilling! You could see why he won seven Primetime Emmy Awards®. Ed had such an enjoyable time, he came back for a second interview.

Ed Asner showcasing his exceptional comic timing. *Photo by Lucie Aleks.*

If my guest is a well-known scream queen from horror movies, you can be sure she'll be screaming during the interview. If it's a YouTuber who unboxes toys, at some point, rest assured I'll have them open a box. If I interview a martial arts star, bodybuilder, professional wrestler, game show host, or dancer, you can bet the audience will see what made them famous—as long as it doesn't involve me being in tights. Actually, come to think of it, I've done that.

This is why James Corden's signature segment, *Carpool Karaoke,* works so well on *The Late Late Show.* You see a famous singer doing what they do best in an everyday setting, without all the bells and whistles of a concert performance. It's an opportunity for them to display their raw talent in a ***compelling*** way that people are drawn to.

When preparing for an interview, remember Pele and the soccer ball…and show them the talent!

TALK BIG TIP

When interviewing someone, and as long as they're physically capable, ask them to demonstrate a skill they're known for. It's often a source of great pride and they'll be happy to share it with you.

MY SECRET PREPARATION

The beauty of preparation is that people don't see it. It's the power you have to make whatever you're working on as artful as possible.

In an interview with Tom Synder, Jerry Lewis talked about a scene from his movie *The Patsy,* where a vase falls from a table and Jerry catches it, just in the nick of time. It's a quick, funny moment yet Jerry says he worked on it for three weeks and broke about four hundred vases until he got it right. That's preparation!

Your preparation can be creative. For my interview with Elliott Gould, I studied his professional life and watched his movies, from classics like *M*A*S*H, The Long Goo•bye,* and *Bob an• Carol an• Te• an• Alice,* to his newer works like *Ocean's Eleven.* I studied his personal life, including his marriage and subsequent divorce from Barbra Streisand. I watched all his interviews, including one where he told Johnny Carson that his biggest complaint is when people think they know him based solely on his films and public life. That stayed with me. With one day left before our interview, I thought, "How can I get a sense of the real Elliott Gould?"

So I took a road trip to his house. You heard me right! My show's coordinator told me he wouldn't be there as he was on set for the TV sitcom *Frien•s,* where he had a recurring role as Jack Geller, the father of David Schwimmer's character, Ross. Outside his home, I walked the grass paths he walked, I saw where he parked his car, I said, "Hello" to his mailman, looked at the trees he saw, and heard the birds he heard. I even picked up a small rock, which I kept in my pocket through show day.

Crazy?

Maybe.

However, the next day when I interviewed him, I felt mentally prepared. I knew details outside of his films and public life. And that helped me. Before the interview even started, I felt ***connected*** to him. It was my secret preparation.

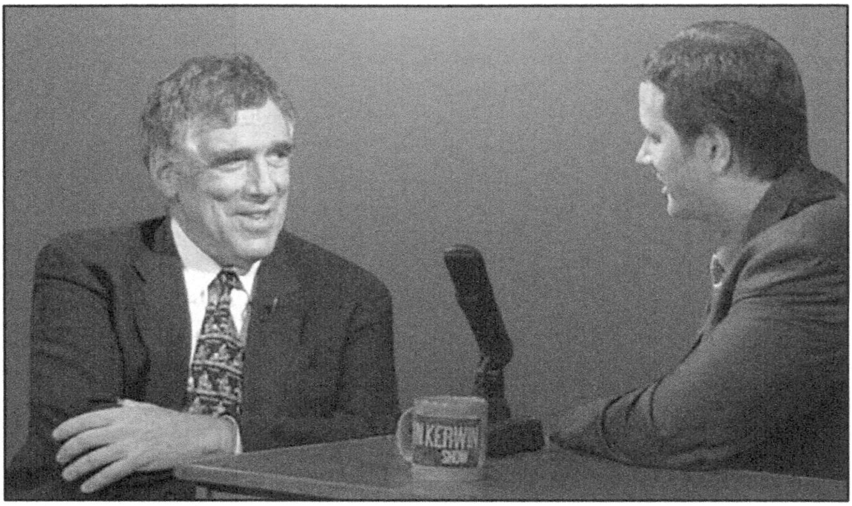

The Actor's Actor Elliott Gould never knew how I secretly prepared for this interview. *Photo by George Kritikos.*

THERE IS NO PERFECTION

When I started interviewing celebrities, I prepared like a madman. Do you know what it's like to watch every episode of *Baywatch*? Maybe you do. Striving for perfection is impossible. Even if you think you've achieved it, chances are the finished product will have no spontaneity and the interview will be a failure anyway.

I loved watching Johnny Carson, yet I remember that down to the week of his retirement, after thirty years he was *still* making mistakes. He was still adjusting to different interview situations, and that's the way it should be. If you're interviewing Kylie Jenner and you ask her to tell a joke, what's more interesting, if she tells the joke perfectly or if she completely screws it up? That's right, embrace disaster!

TALK BIG TIP

Don't aim for perfection. Audiences enjoy interviews that show a side of the celebrity they don't get to see in their movies or TV shows.

Back in the day, the movie studios prohibited their stars from doing television interviews because it risked shattering whatever image they had created. For example, I once read that when the great 1940s movie star Greer Garson appeared on *The Tonight Show,* she arrived on set with the entire interview written out like a script, which she had completely memorized. She was striving for perfection and equated her television interview with one of her film roles.

A celebrity interview should be revealing, and a little risky. I love unpredictability. I've interviewed the actress Sean Young (*Bla•e Runner, Dune, Ace Ventura: Pet Detective*) multiple times, and each time, I never know what she's going to do. I don't know what mood she'll be in or what our dynamic will be, and that's ***compelling***. She gives a great interview. Once again, there is no perfection. A good celebrity interview should be a little messy.

My third interview with the wonderfully unpredictable, Sean Young. *Photo by George Kritikos.*

TALK BIG TIP

Be engaging and a little bit unpredictable when meeting new people. Once while attending a wedding, I asked the bride for her autograph. It was a simple way to honor her, and she loved it! I remember she wrote, *"Thanks for making me feel like a star on the most important day of my life."*

CELEBRITY AUTOBIOGRAPHIES ARE GIFTS FROM THE GODS

If a celebrity has written an autobiography, or a writer has published their authorized biography, see it as a gift from the Gods. I recommend reading them voraciously. These can be the best sources for preparation, and you'll be praised because most interviewers don't read them.

TALK BIG TIP

When a celebrity knows you've read their life story, it immediately creates a *connection.* In their eyes, you're now more respected than most of the other interviewers who didn't take the time to read it.

Another benefit of reading their book is your questions will be better. And you can use direct quotes to dive deeper into other areas of their life.

I once had the good fortune to interview Louis Gossett Jr., the Oscar-winning actor from the film *An Officer an• a Gentleman.* In his book, *An Actor an• a Gentleman,* he writes about his friendship with Marilyn Monroe.

I asked him about this, and he said, "Actually, she wanted to have sex with me. But I said 'No.'"

I said, "I can't believe you turned down Marilyn Monroe. Why?"

He said, "Because back then, Marilyn was the biggest star in the world, and if the public found out that she had sex with a black man, I would've been lynched."

I followed up with, "Do you regret your decision?"

He said, "Actually, yes. If I could go back in time, I would take the gamble."

The audience loved this, and he was an outstanding guest. I don't think he would have discussed any of that with me had I not read his book.

Once again, there is no greater gift for an interviewer than a subject who has written an autobiography or given their blessing to a biographer.

An engaging moment with an officer *and* a gentleman, Louis Gossett, Jr.
Photo by George Kritikos.

TALK BIG TIP

Many people have written blogs or extended entries on their social media pages. Read them and then refer to them when you meet. Oftentimes, you'll make them feel special and establish a real *connection*.

EVEN TARANTINO AND LETTERMAN PREPARE

Director Quentin Tarantino also writes movie reviews, and they're some of the best I've seen since Pauline Kael, who wrote for *The New Yorker* from 1968 to 1991. They're modestly posted on his revival theater site, TheNewBev.com. In 2020, he wrote a review for *Deliverance,* the classic 1972 John Boorman film starring Burt Reynolds. For his review, Tarantino read the novel, *Deliverance,* by James Dickey, and it was obvious he'd seen the film numerous times. He studied it from every angle. That preparation, along with his own writing and directing career, gave him the right to not only show his deep appreciation for this landmark film, but to give his opinion on how it could've been better. Just as Tarantino has earned that right, in order for you to ask a celebrity the questions you've always dreamed of, you must earn the right through preparation.

Before interviewing actor John Savage, I thought, "Who the hell am I to ask 'acting questions' to a supreme thespian who starred opposite Robert De Niro in *The Deer Hunter,* the mesmerizing James Woods in *The Onion Fiel•,* and who starred in the film version of *Hair,* as well as over two hundred other films?"

Well, I'll tell you what gave me that right: Preparation. After the interview, Mr. Savage told my producer, "I thought he was going to make fun of my clothing or something. I had no idea he would be so well-versed in my career. It made me want to do well for him."

When I watch a celebrity interview, I can usually tell within one minute if the interviewer is prepared.

I was invited to an industry taping of *My Next Guest Nee•s No Intro•uction* with David Letterman, where David interviewed actor/comedian

Zach Galifianakis. In preparation for this interview, David had seen every single episode of *Between Two Ferns* twice, and even watched Zach's most obscure films. Not only was Zach impressed, but so was the audience of television professionals in attendance. Could Letterman have decided to "wing it" and still conduct a strong interview? After thirty years of interviewing celebrities, of course! But David is an artist who wants to do his highest level of work, and wisely understands the value of preparation.

Interviewing acclaimed actor John Savage. *Photo by Lucie Aleks.*

MILES DAVIS & THE HUMAN TRUMPET

Questions are the lifeblood of an interview. They may be pre-written, follow-up, spontaneous, and even audience questions.

The power of a good, simple question cannot be overstated. In an interview with Miles Davis, Harry Reasoner asked, "Of all instruments, why do you play the trumpet?"

That's a good, simple question.

Miles Davis replied, "Because I can make the trumpet sound like a human voice."

He then picked up his trumpet and demonstrated. It really *•i•* sound human.

He added, "And this trumpet speaks for me when I can't explain myself in life."

That answer had a profound effect on me. You see, in *my* life, I'm able to best express myself when interviewing. That's when I feel the most free.

I'll give you an example. When my mother died, she wanted to be cremated, so I honored her wish. I then put her ashes inside a wooden box.

Since then, that box has been with me on every celebrity interview. Most of the time, it's in the bookcase behind my desk.

During one interview, an actor asked, "What's in that box?"

After I told him, my staff was in complete shock. All this time, they thought it was just for decoration. Something so personal which I was reluctant to share with my own staff, I was able to discuss freely in front of a nationwide audience.

The revelation I had after hearing Miles Davis answer Harry Reasoner's question was that, for me, interviews are *my* trumpet. That interview took place in 1989, and the first time I saw it, both Miles Davis and Harry Reasoner had passed away. Just another reminder how your questions can resonate well beyond the shelf life of your interviews.

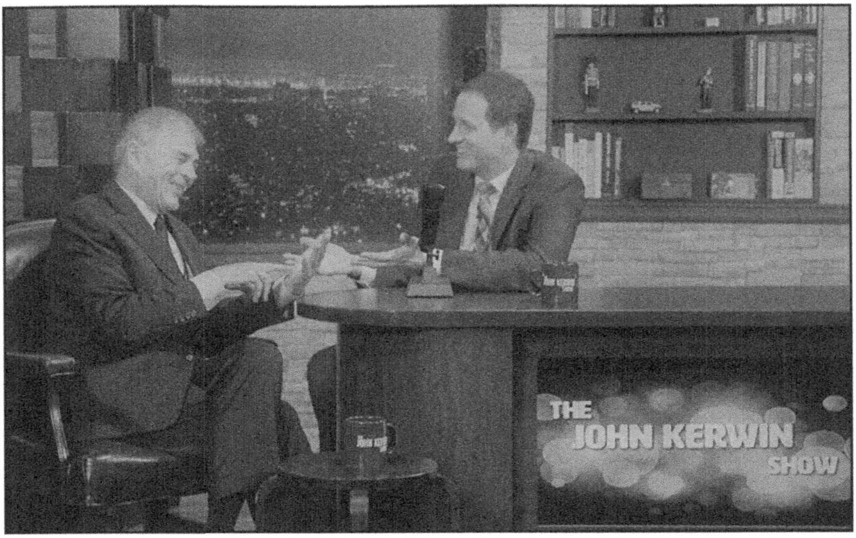

Interviewing the late, great actor Robert Forster, while mom has my back. (Bottom shelf, center box.) *Photo by Lucie Aleks.*

WHY I HATE NOTES

In my opinion, even though many television interviewers use them, notes are a detriment. They force you to read in front of the celebrity, indicating you're not genuinely talking with them. It's hard to build rapport that way, and more than likely, your questions will receive stock answers.

Imagine being on a first date, and in the middle of dinner you start asking questions from a clipboard.

> "What's your favorite movie?"
>
> "Do you like spicy food?"
>
> "Tell me about your first pet."

How would that go over? And no, three-by-five cards don't work any better.

Notes, pads, laptops, and cell phones are all crutches. At a 2020 movie premiere, I saw an interviewer on the red carpet asking questions directly from his iPhone. It looked terrible, and instead of following up with questions based on the celebrity's answers, he just read the next random question from his list. I was half-expecting him to ask, "Do you like strawberry ice cream?"

TALK BIG TIP

Before spending time with family or friends, write out some questions beforehand based on topics you think would be fun to talk about. Then, without using notes, introduce them into the conversation. Magically, you'll be viewed as a great conversationalist.

In 2012, I interviewed the legendary comedian Jonathan Winters at his palatial home in Montecito, California. Halfway through, I excused myself to use the restroom just so I could privately go over my notes and make sure I covered everything. I didn't want to break the illusion of the natural conversation we were having. After the interview, Jonathan said he appreciated the fact that I didn't have prepared questions and he liked how the interview flowed. To further make his point, he said, "I think a lot of the talk show hosts rely too much on prepared questions and answers as opposed to just talking."

That's the impression you want to give.

Interviewing comedy legend Jonathan Winters at his home in Montecito, CA.
Photo by Lucie Aleks.

One of the most dramatic moments in the film *Frost/Nixon* is when David Frost throws down his notepad, looks Richard Nixon in the eye, and asks him a question from the heart.

Former CBS talk show host Craig Ferguson used to rip up a card of questions before each interview to ensure spontaneity.

Don't get me wrong, you probably will need notes to some degree. Especially in the beginning. But as soon as you reach a certain comfort level, I recommend you ween yourself from relying on them. The goal is to cut them out completely. Remember, if an interview is going well, each question should lead to a follow-up question. By actively staying in the moment, your interview will come alive and flow organically.

MEETING CELEBRITIES BACKSTAGE

Going into an interview, don't try to be funny. The last thing a celebrity wants is to feel obligated to laugh at one of your jokes. I've done this before, and it was a disaster. The silence still rings in my ears. The celebrity just looked at me like, "Oh great! *You* want to be the funny one. That's dynamite! Hey, maybe after I bust a gut laughing, you can do a soliloquy from *Hamlet* to prove that you're a better actor too!"

Okay, maybe they weren't thinking that exactly, but it probably wasn't far off.

TALK BIG TIP

When you first meet, your goal is to make the guest feel *comfortable*. Put them at ease so they get a sense you genuinely care about making them look good in the interview.

If the setting is appropriate, offer them coffee or tea, and ask if they need anything else. Check to make sure others are treating them well, too. On a professional level, sometimes I'll tell them that if something's said during the interview that they later regret, just let me know and I'll take it out. Those are the kinds of things that help the guest relax and start trusting you.

USE A PERSON'S CORRECT TITLE

One way to create ***comfort*** is by getting a person's job title or status correct. This includes:

- Politicians
- Members of the clergy
- Military officers
- Doctors
- Judges
- Royalty

To name a few. They worked very hard (or paid off a lot of people) to get that title, so respect it! If you're not sure of their title, even though you prepared, ask them in a sincere manner how they'd like to be addressed.

When first meeting Ben Kingsley, I said, "It's a pleasure to meet you, Mr. Kingsley."

He glared at me and said, "It's Sir Ben!"

After absorbing that, I replied, "My apologies, Sir Ben. Feel free to call me Idiot John."

It felt like mountains were being moved as he cracked a smile. (I resisted the urge to ask if his niece called him Uncle Ben.)

DON'T PREPARE IN A VACUUM

Despite all of my research, sometimes I'll tell people about a celebrity I'm interviewing, and they'll provide a better question than anything I've prepared. In preparation, you sometimes miss the obvious things people want to know about the star.

Many times, the celebrity is involved in some project that means little to you but is very important to other people.

Previous to interviewing Michael Jai White, I studied his performances in *Spawn, Tyson,* and *Kill Bill 2* (his scene was deleted). On the day of the interview, I kept hearing people talk about something called *Black Dynamite.* Turns out, Michael was the star of that show, which was a hit animated series I'd glossed over in my research. More people were interested in *Black Dynamite* than anything else I'd prepared. From that day on, I started talking with everyone I could prior to my interviews to learn what *they* found most interesting about the celebrity.

I first interviewed Michael Jai White for a magazine profile and that went so well, he joined me as a guest on my talk show. A 7-time black belt, you don't want to tangle with *him*! *Photo by Lucie Aleks.*

EXCEPTIONS TO PREPARING

There are exceptions to everything, including preparation. On *The Tonight Show with Jay Leno,* I always thought Jay's best interviews were with comedians. While he might have been less at ease talking with Meryl Streep, he was confident with comics, because he was one of them and understood their life and art. He could relate to with them, tease them, ask inside questions, riff with them, and even call them out when they were reworking old jokes. Sometimes he even managed to get to the heart of who they really were, a rarity on late night talk shows. He was so familiar with the world of comedy that he didn't need to prepare—his preparation for those interviews came from decades of working the road and hundreds of TV appearances. This gave him the gravitas to be fully confident and free when talking with stand-ups. For those interviews, Jay needed no preparation.

You may be friends with a celebrity and because of that, the interview will be rich with comradery. The danger with "friendship interviews" is that sometimes they can get "too inside" and leave the audience feeling left out. But generally speaking, it's a huge advantage to personally know a celebrity before interviewing them. When you have that rare relationship, your understanding of each other and shared experiences becomes the preparation. Because what could be more ***compelling*** than that level of ***comfort*** and ***connection?***

I remember being so excited when Eddie Murphy appeared on *The Arsenio Hall Show.* Arsenio and Eddie's friendship led to an on-air kinship rarely seen.

Exceptions aside, preparation enables you to be ready, willing, and able to interview anyone.

THE MANY BENEFITS OF FOCUS GROUPS

If you really want to up your game, take your preparation a step further and put together a focus group.

When I did my kids' television show, I'd always ask the five-to eleven-year-olds in the studio audience, "Next week my guests are so and so. What should I ask them?" This led to 150 kids yelling out suggestions. And their questions were fantastic! They were far better than anything I could come up with because they were the target audience for those celebrities. Those girls and boys became amazing focus groups.

Be inventive when initiating your focus group. Let's say you have a podcast and two hundred fans follow you. Right there you have a potential focus group. You can reach out to them and ask, "I'm interviewing YouTube star, Pamela Swing. What would you like to know about her?" In addition to engaging the audience, you can be sure they'll tune in to your podcast to hear if their questions will be asked.

TALK BIG TIP

Join online fan clubs for the celebrity and ask its members for questions, so long as they're also in your show or podcast's demographic.

"Fan" questions can get a little tricky. If I'm interviewing a hockey star, I may not want questions from hardcore hockey fans because they'll be too technical—the kind of questions you'd hear on a sports podcast. I want to know what the people watching my show want to know about that hockey player.

Prepping to interview Kathy Griffin, my focus group consisted of everyone who followed me on social media and watched my show.

"What should I ask Kathy Griffin?"

I wanted to hear everything—what they liked and didn't like about her. I wanted to know what projects of hers excited them as opposed to those that didn't resonate. One thing I found out was that, like me, many of my viewers loved Quentin Tarantino films. Kathy dated Quentin during the filming of *Pulp Fiction,* and she even had a small part in that movie. When I reached out to my focus group, I got over a hundred questions about Kathy in *Pulp Fiction.* If not for them, I probably would've asked just one question on that subject, then moved on. Conversely, I'd written a whole bunch of questions about her TV show *Su••enly Susan,* but my focus group told me that they weren't as interested in that. So I cut those questions out.

Another thing I found out was my viewers didn't like it when she was too gossipy. So before the interview, I asked Kathy if she could refrain from attacking celebrities, and she said, "Of course. If you don't go there, I won't go there."

Interviewing the inherently funny Kathy Griffin. *Photo by George Kritikos.*

She totally kept her word. She was extremely funny, yet very respectful, and the feedback from my audience was that of all the Kathy Griffin interviews, mine was their favorite. That came as no surprise, as the interview was tailored especially for them.

TALK BIG TIP

A focus group should not replace your research on the celebrity, only add to it. Remember, their questions should consist of what *your* audience would want to know about the celebrity. That, coupled with what *you* want to know, will lead to the best possible interview.

When prepping for an interview you're like Sherlock Holmes studying a murder suspect. You want to know all you can about them. Don't just go on Wikipedia and write up ten questions. For one, Wikipedia is often full of errors, and the celebrity will probably call you out, making you look like a bad interviewer.

Prepare thoroughly and go the extra mile by cultivating focus groups. If you ever feel like skipping past the research, remind yourself that this is your dream job, and the grunt work is a small price to pay.

6 CONDUCTING YOUR INTERVIEW

As shown in Chapter 4, the **Three C's** are: making the celebrity ***comfortable***, ***connecting*** with them, and making the interview ***compelling.*** If you have these three things, your interview will be a success.

COMFORT

For a TV studio interview, here's what I do:

- Find out from the publicist or manager the celebrity's favorite snacks and drinks. When they'll arrive, they instantly feel at home.
- Hire makeup people who are not only talented, but really good at making the celebrity feel special and excited about being there.

- Have a small, yet thoughtful, gift waiting.
- Make sure their team is treated like royalty.

It bears repeating: During the interview, you want to ensure your guest is ***comfortable***.

Once while interviewing an actor who seemed very agitated, rather than ignore it, I asked if everything was okay.

He said, "Actually, I really have to pee."

The studio audience laughed.

Then I said, "So do I."

We then excused ourselves and went to the men's room. A few minutes later, we returned and took a big theatrical bow. This got huge applause. We then complimented each other's manhood, which got even more laughs, and then proceeded with the interview. He went from being terribly uncomfortable to totally relaxed and ready to give his best effort.

Again: Always make sure the celebrity is ***comfortable***— before, during, and after the interview.

TALK BIG TIP

Sometimes a simple smile will make a person feel *comfortable*. Or, if they appear nervous, say, "I don't know why these events always make me nervous." Now they have an ally. Whether it's finding common ground or the nearest restroom, look for ways to relax them and you'll be on your way to a solid *connection*.

CONNECT

Many years ago, I was watching *The Rosie O'Donnell Show* for the first time and she did a celebrity interview that blew me away. Rarely had I seen a host so ***connected*** with a guest—like they were best friends. The interview ended with them high-fiving and hugging. I thought, "That's an unusual ***connection***. They must be close."

Then Rosie introduced her next guest . . . and it was the exact same thing! I realized, "Oh, I get it. That's something Rosie's really good at."

The best way to ***connect*** with a celebrity is through doing research and finding the connective tissue between the two of you. The interview becomes like a conversation because it seems the two of you have a lot in common.

When I first met Teri Hatcher, the *Desperate Housewives* star, I discovered we both love the movie *Tootsie.* We started discussing our favorite scenes, quoted dialogue from the film, and very quickly found our ***connection***.

Go online and check out the episode of the podcast *You Up with Nikki Glaser,* featuring an interview with comedian Hannah Berner. It truly illustrates a great ***connection*** with a guest. These two funny women chat like they're in a sorority, talking about life, dating and how they both had sex with a mutual boyfriend...thus calling themselves "Eskimo Sisters." The interview is so much fun you'll want to check out other episodes of *You Up,* watch Berner's show *Summer House,* then listen to her podcast *Berning in Hell.* That's the effect a strong ***connection*** has.

In 2009, I interviewed Tom Bergeron, the host of *Dancing with the Stars.* At the time, he was making the rounds promoting his autobiography, *I'm Hosting as Fast as I Can.* I read his book beforehand and asked detailed questions about it. This impressed him and we started talking about how I was once a champion contestant on *Hollywood Squares*, a game show he hosted. We also discussed how early in his career, he hosted a talk show in Boston, much like mine, and I told him how that show influenced my work. All of these things led to us having a strong ***connection***. In fact, sometime after our interview, we got together for lunch and had a great time.

Finding out the things you have in common with your guest is the best way to develop a strong ***connection***.

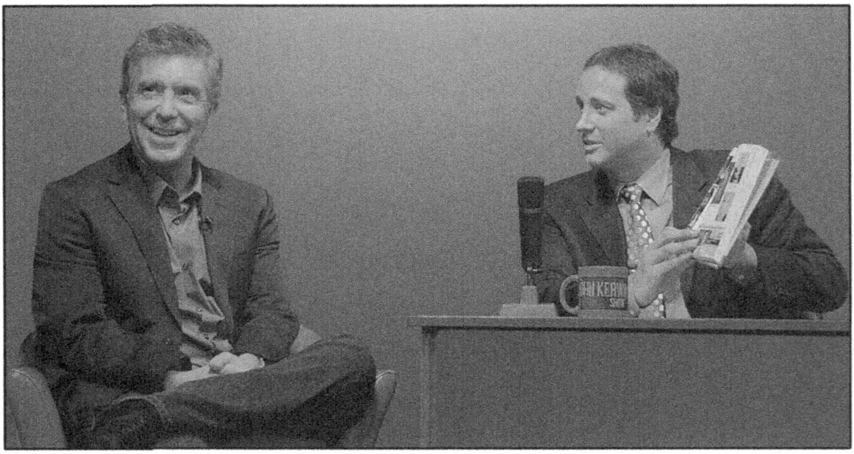

Tom Bergeron and I share a laugh. *Photo by George Kritikos*

COMPEL

Many factors can make your interviews ***compelling***. What's fascinating for one person might not be for another. My Aunt Betty has a collection of origami elephants. Let's just say, not everyone shares her passion. A K-pop star might blow away a teenager but completely bore an octogenarian.

A ***compelling*** conversation can be very funny or very poignant. Comedians like Hannibal Buress, John Mulaney, or Bill Burr, when they're "killing," are highly ***compelling***. Once on *The Tonight Show,* actor Jimmy Stewart brought the audience to tears with a poem he wrote about his beloved dog, Beau. That, too, was ***compelling***.

Your guest may give a captivating performance like Ariana Grande's show-stopping musical impressions of Christina Aguilera and Celine Dion.

Maybe you'll snag a revealing interview like Robin Roberts getting Selma Blair to open up about her MS diagnosis.

A ***compelling*** interview must bring out moments of:

- Exhilaration
- Anger
- Laughter
- Sadness
- Regret
- Or other emotions that really touch and influence people

Compelling moments can emanate from a major life event, like a marriage proposal, a star's comeback from rehab, or an announcement that they're coming out as gay, transitioning, or other self-identifying change.

Obviously, you don't want to ask or do something to upset the celebrity or make them uncomfortable. But asking yourself, "What's the most ***compelling*** thing this person can do during the interview" can lead to some great moments.

Growing up, I loved the TV show *Dallas,* so when I landed an interview with the show's star, Larry Hagman, I asked myself that very question, "What's the most ***compelling*** thing he can do during this interview?" Well... his character J.R. Ewing was perhaps the meanest, nastiest character in television history, and I wanted Larry to do something as J.R.

So during the interview, I created the scenario where J.R. Ewing found out I had sex with his wife, Sue Ellen. He summoned me into his "office," where I arrogantly lit up a cigarette and started smoking. What followed was Larry Hagman acting as J.R. Ewing and giving me a tongue-lashing in the most wonderfully despicable way. He was truly ***compelling*** and it's one of my all-time favorite interviewing moments.

Larry Hagman scolding me as J.R. Ewing from *Dallas*. *Photo by George Kritikos*

One of my first memorable interviews was with Academy Award-winning actress Cloris Leachman. By the time we sat down, Cloris had been in over one hundred films, and of course starred in *The Mary Tyler Moore Show* and a spin-off of that show, *Phyllis.*

As the interview concluded, I gave her a friendly on-air kiss. Her response was, "C'mon, let's do a *real* kiss."

The studio audience cheered, and I suddenly had Cloris Leachman's tongue down my throat. When it was over, I mimed smoking a cigarette, but I was truly in a state of shock.

Then she whispered to me, "Oh, relax, I did the same bit on Comedy Central with John Stamos."

Apparently, she had a thing for guys named John. And that thing was her tongue.

To me, "***compelling***" is the audience hanging on every word. It's when your spouse is standing naked in front of the TV, and you're waving them out of the way.

An unforgettable moment with Academy Award-winning actress Cloris Leachman. *Photo by George Kritikos.*

START OFF IN THE MOMENT

In 2011, I interviewed Grammy Award®-winning composer Charles Fox. In addition to creating some of the greatest TV theme songs of all-time, for shows like *Happy Days, The Love Boat, Mon•ay Night Football,* and countless others, he also composed the number one song *Killing Me Softly.*

As he was taking a moment to get situated, I started singing, "Strumming my face with his fingers..." while looking right into his eyes.

It gave him an opportunity to get big laughs by saying, "You're no Robert Flack!" It also led to him telling a great anecdote about that song, which kicked things off nicely.

That's another secret: Never be afraid to play straight man and give your guest the spotlight.

Regardless, always deal with the reality of the opening moment.

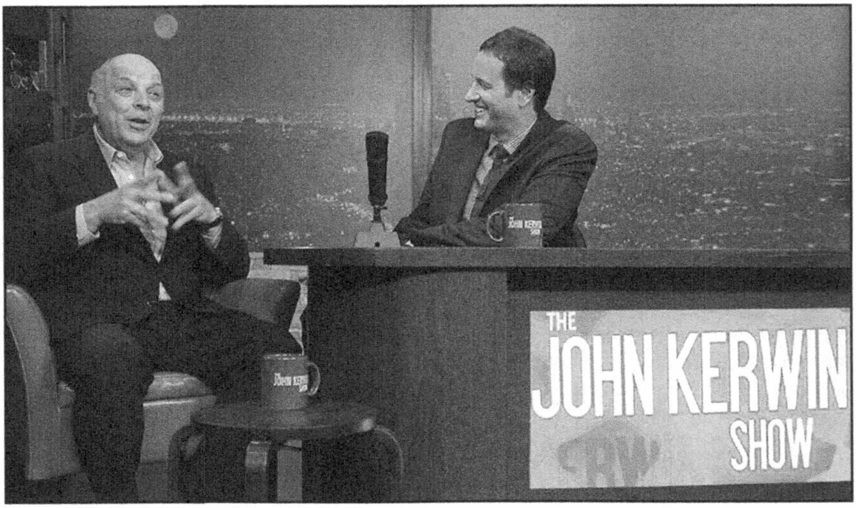

Interviewing multi-Grammy®-winning composer, Charles Fox. *Photo by Lucie Aleks*

I once saw an actress enter and sit down for an interview holding a pet monkey. And the interviewer's first question was, "So, tell us about your new movie?"

Tell us about your new movie??!! What about the monkey?? That monkey should've flung his feces right at that interviewer. Of course, he probably would've just ignored it and asked her the next question.

Embrace surprises, as they provide some of the most memorable moments from an interview. And always begin in the moment.

TALK BIG TIP

Always begin an interview in the moment. Even if it's just talking about their outfit, their drive to the studio, or the chair they're sitting on. Something other than just going right into question number one.

BEARING GIFTS

A gift is a great icebreaker. It doesn't have to be overly presentational—just something gift wrapped that can be hidden in your pocket. Giving a present upon meeting someone creates an interesting dynamic. First of all, everyone loves gifts. It's a basic truth of show business. No matter how rich someone is, they still love freebies.

Secondly, there's the built-in drama of, "What's this person giving me?" As they open it, there's hopefully a positive reaction, then an instant ***connection*** to you. The gift should be based on your research and preferably something they rarely, if ever, get. I remember reading a rider from Carrot Top's contract that said, in big letters, "Please no carrot cake! It's still not funny!" Be creative or the gift can backfire.

As I write this, a friend is trying to get me a meeting with Larry King. Larry and I are both from New York City, so as a gift, I got him a "Spaldeen" ball. That's the red rubber ball, made by Spalding®, that every kid from Larry's generation played with in the streets of New York City from the 1950s onward. They're not easy to find, and I'm guessing that, like me, he hasn't seen one in years. That gift lends itself to talking about our similar backgrounds as boys growing up in New York. It's a gift that packs a sentimental punch and creates ***connection.***

Fred Rogers, TV's "Mr. Rogers," wasn't usually thought of as a great interviewer, but he was. He also understood the power of gift-giving. I once saw him look into the camera and say, "Can I give you something? The day I knew I'd visit with you, I was walking on the beach and I found this shell."

He then took a seashell from his pocket, rubbed some water on it and said, "If you put a little water on it, it gets even more beautiful. And I keep thinking...that has something to do with life. That tears and sweat often bring out the best in us."

The riskiest gift I ever gave was for an interview I did on Mother's Day. Through my research it was revealed that, like me, my guest had lost his mother that year. Prior to the show I gave him a box of chocolates along with a Mother's Day card. Inside the card I'd pasted pictures of our mothers side by side, with the dates of their passing.

Inside the card I wrote, "Tonight, our mothers' spirits will be with us." The interview went particularly well, and afterward the makeup artist told me she had to reapply his makeup because he was so touched by the gift.

I learned the importance of gift giving when a celebrity gave *me* a gift. It was the effort more than the value. When Nancy Cartwright (the voice of Bart Simpson) was a guest on my show, she brought a giant cake she'd baked for me. It had my name on it with a decoration of a guitar, which she'd found out I enjoyed playing. It was very thoughtful, and afterward, we gave a slice to everyone in the studio audience and to my staff.

The voice of Bart Simpson, Nancy Cartwright, surprises me with a cake. And I just expected her to say, "Eat My Shorts!" *Photo by George Kritikos.*

So as you can see, gifts are a great way to establish rapport, and strengthen the ***connection*** between you and your guest.

TALK BIG TIP

I have a friend who always brings some silly toy or conversation piece when we meet for lunch. It's usually some cheap novelty item she found, yet it always gives us something to talk about. Think about bringing a fun, little gift the next time you get together with a friend or date.

THE SECRET ED MCMAHON TAUGHT ME ABOUT INTERVIEWING

In 2004, Johnny Carson's longtime sidekick, Ed McMahon, extended an invitation to his palatial home to give some advice to me and comedian Jimmy Brogan, who was going to be my sidekick on a new talk show.

As Ed introduced himself, I was taken by how immaculately dressed he was, even in casual wear. My extensive research allowed me to start off by complimenting his attire and mentioning how it's no surprise that he was once on Mr. Blackwell's Best Dressed List in Hollywood. Ed gave his familiar laugh and then thanked me for giving his assistant a chew toy gift for his beloved sheepdog, Muffin, who was quietly enjoying it in a nearby room.

The three of us sat on a couch and the irony wasn't lost at how Ed spent countless television hours sitting on a similar couch, arguably the most well-known couch in America.

Later, Ed showed us his full radio studio which he had built-in to his home, mentioning that he'd just finished an interview with Kevin Costner. As I looked around, I saw endless framed photographs on the walls with Ed next to presidents, astronauts, and every major star from the past four decades. Interestingly, there wasn't a single photo of Johnny Carson, which made sense, for this was Ed McMahon's house, and here *he* was king.

It's surreal how this meeting turned into an interview with me asking questions and Jimmy chiming in with funny and insightful comments. Jimmy was acquainted with Ed, as he'd been a guest on *The Tonight Show Starring Johnny Carson* seven times. It's one of my regrets that negotiations fell through and Jimmy and I never got to work together. I would have to be satisfied with this meeting, which was so ultra-professional, it felt as if cameras should've been recording us.

Ed talked freely about his comradery with Johnny and the delicate balance between host and sidekick when interviewing. Much of their success as a team was learned through trial and error, spanning over hundreds of television hours. However, he said it's important to note that they genuinely liked each other and had been friends for decades. In fact, he disclosed that he recently had lunch with Johnny in Malibu and the waitress's name happened to be "Monica," which led to Johnny rattling off Monica Lewinsky jokes non-stop throughout the meal.

Then Ed stressed his most important lesson. He said the secret to Johnny's interviewing success was that he was genuinely curious about the people he interviewed. That may sound simple, yet it's essential. Ed watched Johnny conduct hundreds of interviews and witnessed how that curiosity galvanized interview after interview, time after time.

I'll never forget Ed looking me in the eyes and saying, "It's something to always remember: Be curious."

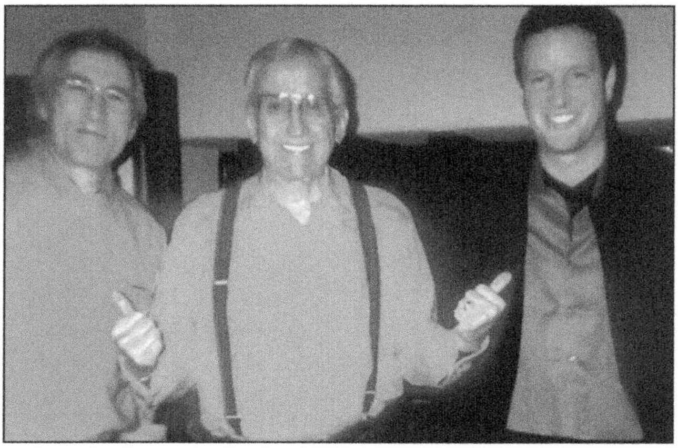

At Ed McMahon's house with Jimmy Brogan. *Photo by Stacy Altman.*

BE CURIOUS

Think of when you go on a date and you really like the other person. You want to know everything about them, including:

- Where they're from
- Where they went to school
- If they have siblings
- What they do for fun

Access that same curiosity when interviewing.

I interviewed kid stars from Disney and Nickelodeon TV shows for a year straight. I honestly didn't know any of them. However, I made sure to remain curious about their lives because I was once a child, and it was like suddenly I was hanging out with the most popular kids in school. I tried imagining how I would feel as a kid interviewing them—how exciting that'd be, what I'd ask them, and what I'd want to know.

TALK BIG TIP

Practice being genuinely curious about the lives of the everyday people you meet. Whether rideshare drivers or store clerks, you'll be amazed at what you can learn.

LISTENING

I once had the good fortune of interviewing two-time Oscar-nominated and Cannes Best Actor award-winner Bruce Dern. I asked simple questions and Bruce gave fantastic answers. I followed up with another simple question or moved on to another topic. Each time he had wonderful answers and anecdotes.

As the interview was ending, I could feel my stomach turn. I realized that I didn't get any laughs or add any interesting comments during our conversation.

But then he ended our interview by saying, "You know, I've gotta tell ya. I've been interviewed by all the usual people starting with Johnny Carson. And John Kerwin has a tremendous talent that is very rare. If he feels that someone has a little bit of game, he lets them go. And even though he's got all those questions prepared, he lets you dance and then has the ability, by his quietness, of dancing with you. And ya know why? Because he's got a gift. That's talent, and very few people have that."

I was in a state of shock. Then it dawned on me—by simply staying in the moment and listening with intent, I'd done some of my best work. His compliment changed my life.

I learned an important lesson during my interview with Bruce Dern. *Photo by George Kritikos.*

REMEMBERING

Another important part of listening is remembering. When a celebrity is asked a question and then goes off on a tangent, it's your responsibility to go back and get the first question answered. Otherwise the audience feels cheated. How many times have you watched an interview and they finally ask the right question and then it doesn't get answered? It's infuriating, right?

It's even worse when the celebrity says, "What was I just talking about?" and the interviewer doesn't remember. That's when I flip to something more entertaining. Like C-SPAN.

Again, my mother taught me this the hard way. If she was talking about an argument that she'd had with her friend, and then the phone rang, she'd take the call and then come back and ask me to review exactly where we were in the conversation. If I didn't know . . . WHACK!

FOLLOW-UP QUESTIONS

Follow-up questions come from active listening. When you ask a question, the answer will dictate your next question. For example, if you ask, "What was your most memorable audition?"

And they answer, "The time I took out a loaded gun."

Your next question should *not* be, "And who's your favorite actor?"

Your follow-up questions must be about the gun.

"Why did you do that?"

"What did they do when you took out the gun?"

"Did you get in trouble?"

"Did you get the part?"

If you go on a first date and ask, "How did your last relationship end?"

And they say, "We both ended up in jail."

Would your next question be, "Do you like sushi?"

THE SPARK

A spark is the thing in life that the celebrity is passionate about. By tapping into this, they'll open up during the interview. Different people have different sparks. A question that's been asked a thousand times no longer excites them. For example, asking a celebrity how they got cast in their TV series will most likely get a strong response during the show's initial success. But ask that same question a few years later and it may just get a sigh or a dull retelling of the facts. It may even get the dreaded, "I auditioned and got it" answer.

Do your detective work to find their spark. I once interviewed a star who showed up and was clearly a very guarded person. He was a tough-guy actor and was none too excited about our interview. Then I noticed he had on a tie clip with a little airplane on it. I pointed to it and asked, "Do you like to fly?"

He lit up like a Christmas tree! He started talking about his love of flying and how he felt the most alive when he was alone in the sky. "It's like I'm at one with God," he said.

His passion for flying was a thing of beauty, and because I'd found his spark, the rest of the interview was a snap.

(FYI, "talking points" are usually not your guest's spark—they're the publicist's thoughts on how certain questions can help the celebrity's career).

Many times, the celebrity hands you the spark. They might say (or their people will tell you) they want to talk about their charity, their Off-Broadway play, or even their favorite hobby.

Actor Michael Gross and I once sat down for an interview. While looking into his background, I discovered his spark was model trains. He's a collector and knows everything about them. So we discussed model trains. Going into that interview, I was eager to talk about Michael J. Fox and *Family Ties*, yet the best part of the interview came from his passion for his hobby.

***Family Ties*'actor, Michael Gross, is a model train enthusiast and shared his "spark" with our audience.** *Photo by Lucie Aleks*

One celebrity I interviewed had a new Las Vegas slot machine based on him. So guess what his spark was? Simple questions followed, such as,

"How did you get your own slot machine?"

"Have you played it?"

"Did you win?"

"How big is your cut of the profits?"

Those "spark-based" questions opened the door to him giving a wonderful interview.

One particularly rough beginning to an interview came during a session with a child celebrity. She kept giving one-word answers to every question. I quickly ditched everything and just asked, "What do you like to do for fun?"

She said, "Scrapbooking."

I asked, "What's that?"

"You paste souvenirs of memories and put them in a book."

"Oh, can you teach me?"

"Well, we don't have supplies."

I asked the parents in the studio audience if anyone had scrapbooking supplies. Someone gave us a few stickers and glitter. Then we got a pair of scissors and some paper from my office. I had someone yank off her nameplate hanging on the door of the green room. We decorated that and pasted it on paper. Suddenly, she was animated and happy we were scrapbooking together. Her newfound energy transformed the interview. She asked for my autograph and I agreed, but she wanted me to do it like people do at the Chinese Theatre in Hollywood. So I took off my shoes and socks and dipped my hands and feet in glitter. I then imprinted them on paper and signed it. It was so much fun! All the while I was asking her questions about her TV show and she talked up a storm.

I'd found her spark.

TALK BIG TIP

When talking with someone new, ask questions to try and figure out their spark. Trust me, you'll know when you've found it.

PLUGGING AND A JAMES BOND MOMENT

Promoting your guest's projects is an art. Commonly referred to as "plugging," for most guests, it's the main reason you got the interview. That's critical to remember. While you certainly don't want to turn the interview into an infomercial, you also can't have the attitude of, "Oh, great, I have to squeeze in this damn plug." The attitude should be, "Here's a way I can return the favor of having the privilege of interviewing this celebrity. Here's a way I can further create a ***connection*** with this person."

As I pointed out in Chapter 5 on Preparation, if their plug is for a book, read it! If it's for a movie, see it! This keeps you from turning into a big phony when giving the plug. My strong recommendation is to be honest.

Don't say a movie or book is spectacular if you don't think so. The audience will know you're being disingenuous, and you'll lose their trust. Again, be honest. Now you might be asking, "What if the movie sucked?" Well, the way to handle that is to find something about your guest's performance that you liked. Call attention to that. Good things exist in almost all movies, TV shows, books, etc. If you don't do your preparation, then you're left with either giving a perfunctory, generic plug, or having to lie and endorse something you never read or watched.

My favorite way to plug is creatively integrating their project into the interview. This makes the plug more memorable and, if the plug ties in with your guest's "spark," it helps build a stronger bond between the two of you. And their publicist will be thrilled.

Jayde Nicole was a cast member on the MTV show, *The Hills.* She also happened to be 2008's *Playboy* Playmate of the Year®. Jayde was on my show to promote a poker program, and after discussing her career, she mentioned how she loved to gamble. This was the perfect time to do a plug for her, so I offered her a bet. Someone on our staff had a deck of cards and I suggested we play one hand of "5 card draw" poker. If she won, I'd promote her poker videos on the next five shows.

She asked, "Great, but what if *you* win?"

I said, "Then right here on television, we kiss."

The audience cheered.

She said, "It's a bet!"

The cards were dealt. She drew a strong hand of kings and nines. I asked her to show the hand to the camera. Smiling proudly, she was certain she'd won, until I showed *my* hand, which had 3 aces. The audience went wild and what followed was (no shade to Cloris Leachman) my all-time favorite on-camera kiss.

After that, I came clean and explained that when I asked her to show her poker hand to the camera, I switched 3 of my cards for aces, which I'd planted earlier under the seat of my chair. She laughed and said that it was her first kiss since breaking up with Brody Jenner on *The Hills.* I pointed out that since I'd tricked her, I'd promote her product on the next five shows, which of course I did. Jayde was a great sport and gave a terrific interview.

Did I mention that interviewing celebrities is fun?

Promoting a celebrity's projects and/or products is an integral part of being an interviewer. For example, you can visit JaydeNicole.com for her ever-growing line of eco-friendly products. *Photo by George Kritikos.*

DID YOU GET MY MOVIE?

I can't tell you how many times I've heard an actor on a podcast or on a TV show ask the interviewer, "I had my movie sent over, did you get it?"

And the interviewer says, "Yes, I got it. I just haven't had a chance to watch it."

That'll be the last time that actor does that show. How would you feel? Would you be able to open up to that person? Would you recommend him to your celebrity friends?

Not finding the time to watch your guest's movie (or read their book) is one of the most egregious things an interviewer can do. Even if it isn't good, it should be your top priority. And believe me, the worse the project is, the more they appreciate it.

The good news is that by doing the right thing and watching their movie, you build a strong rapport, can talk in specifics about the film, and gain their trust so they give you the best interview possible.

CHILD MODE

I was one of those kids who asked a million questions and drove their teachers nuts. If they said, "Today we're going to learn about the sun," my hand would go up.

At 10 years old, ready to ask more questions.

"Why is it called the sun?"

"How hot is the sun?"

"How far away is it?"

"Could we live on the sun?"

"How old is the sun?"

"Why shouldn't you look at the sun?"

"Why do we get suntans?"

Teachers hated me. But here's how that way of thinking can help you with your interviewing.

I once got a job interviewing celebrities on the 18th hole of a charity golf tournament. I knew nothing about golf and was not going to pretend that I did—so I went into child mode. I asked simple questions such as,

> "Why is it called golf?"
>
> "Why is the ball that size?"
>
> "Why are there 18 holes?"
>
> "Why do you wear those clothes?"

I was genuinely interested, and the celebrities gave funny and interesting answers. Robin Williams had the best line: "Golf is a sport where white men get to dress like black pimps."

TALK BIG TIP

The next time you get into a conversation with someone who has specialized knowledge, and you haven't had time to prepare, go into child mode. Ask simple questions and marvel at how much you learn.

THE UNIQUE QUESTION TRAP

Many interviewers try to ask questions that the celebrity has never, ever been asked before. It's almost like the goal is for them to say, "That's a great question. You're really good!" The truth is, when they say that, more often than not, it's a stall tactic to give them time to come up with an answer. Having totally unique questions is an interesting goal, but the most important thing is to get the celebrity to open up and give you the most ***compelling*** interview possible.

Sometimes a line of totally unique questioning can lull the celebrity into a quiet, cerebral place, which can make the interview slow-moving and introspective rather than emotional and visceral.

An interviewer once asked Lucille Ball if being the star of *I Love Lucy* created jealousy from her husband. Lucy said, "No, because Desi Arnaz was the star of the show. He was the 'I' in *I Love Lucy.*" This answer, to a common question, revealed so much about their relationship. She knew that it wasn't easy for a man to play second fiddle to his wife. In that answer you could see Lucy's compassion and love for her husband.

While interviewing Timothy Bottoms, the star of movies like *The Paper Chase* and *The Last Picture Show,* I asked him the simple question, "Is there a film role that you turned down and later regretted?"

He took a long pause and then said, "I turned down the Richard Dreyfuss role in *Jaws.*"

There was an audible gasp from the audience. I remember hearing one person say, "Ohhh mannn!" Timothy then discussed how he would have played that role, which was fascinating.

In a 1963 interview with Martin Luther King Jr., David Susskind asked him, "Do you consider it a miracle that you haven't been murdered?"

King responded that he has often pondered why there has been no actual attempt to kill him. It's a chilling interviewing moment.

Sometimes a simple, straightforward question can produce an answer that will stay with people for generations.

THE WILD QUESTION

For the celebrity who's been asked the same things over and over, sometimes an off-beat question can lead to fun and creative answers. This differs from the unique question, which is normally serious and thought provoking.

The answers to wild questions can end up being the best part of the interview. But understand that there is a risk. Barbara Walters once famously asked a celebrity, "If you were a tree, which would you be?" and she got satirized for years over that. Still, I think it's worth the gamble.

TALK BIG TIP

Make a list of 10 wild questions, and practice asking them in your daily encounters. I once asked a librarian, "What's the strangest thing you ever found inside a returned book?" She said, "A slice of cheese. And the book was *Stuart Little.*"

Here are a few wild questions I've asked:

Do you ever talk to yourself?

Have you ever been bitten by a dog?

Are you double-jointed?

What's your favorite Stevie Wonder song?

As a kid, how would you enter a swimming pool?

If you had to describe your childhood with one smell, what would it be?

What's your favorite article of clothing in your wardrobe?

When was the last time you laughed so hard your stomach hurt?

WHAT IF YOU'RE NERVOUS?

If you feel yourself being nervous, try putting your attention on the guest, and listen. Sometimes when a guest gives a long answer, there's a tendency for your mind to drift and think about the next question or about all the people watching. Fight this! Stay in the moment and listen to your guest with intent. If you're still nervous, just try and relax. I guarantee that as you interview more, the nerves will diminish.

Being a little nervous can actually help you. Sometimes I'll listen to a podcast and the hosts are so relaxed, it feels like they're falling asleep. And I'm right behind them. If you're too chill, this will cause the celebrity to mirror your lack of energy, and the interview may be missing excitement or energy. That's why I love a TV studio audience. It puts positive pressure on the interview.

This has never been more evident than during 2020's COVID-19 Pandemic. Devoid of a studio audience, talk shows, stand-up comedians and variety shows like *Satur•ay Night Live* found it challenging to recreate the same dynamic as performing in front of a live studio audience. So a level of nervousness should be embraced. If you're concerned about being *severely* nervous, just remember that repetition is the cure. I was always scared to death on the first day of school. Yet, within a week, I was pulling the fire alarm.

A TRICK DICK CAVETT TAUGHT ME

In 2004, I was hosting a new talk show and had the honor of being introduced by the legendary Dick Cavett, who also happened to be my first guest.

Backstage, I confided to Dick that I was nervous.

He said, "It might help if we cursed each other out." Even though I'd just met him, I loved the idea and quickly agreed.

So he called me an asshole.

I answered back, "Fuck you."

Back and forth we went, and it really worked to relax me. I'll never forget the look on my producer's face as he walked by. Now *he* was the nervous one.

Who would've guessed what happened backstage? Talk show host extraordinaire, Dick Cavett. *Photo by George Kritikos.*

DON'T LET NERVES DESTROY YOUR DREAM

A former girlfriend of mine once told me the story of her music career. She was a local singer in Hollywood and was finally getting some attention. One night, the opportunity of a lifetime came her way—filling in for another singer who was sick with the flu. It wasn't just any venue, either, it was the Hollywood Bowl, which seats an audience of 17,500.

Some of the greatest musical acts in history, including the Beatles, have performed there. It was a huge break, and the music industry's most powerful executives would be in attendance. That night, prepping to go onstage, she looked out into the sold-out crowd.

And panicked.

She ran off the stage, got in her car, and drove away from the gig. As she told me this story, tears rolled down her face. By far, it was her biggest regret in life. She never sang again.

It's a sad story that I never wanted to happen to me, and I hope it never happens to you. I can't tell you how many times I've been scared out of my mind going into some interviewing situation. But I always summon the courage to never, ever run away.

DON'T FAWN OVER THE CELEBRITY

As an interviewer, you must remain professional. Don't say things like, "Oh my God, thank you soooooo much! I'm so excited to meet you! I can't believe this is happening!" You'll lose all credibility and respect; worse, the celebrity might even walk.

It's like a guy on a first date saying, "I can't believe I'm on a date with you! You're so incredibly gorgeous. I feel dizzy. I think I'm falling in love!"

As comedian Wendy Liebman says, "They'll leave skidmarks."

As a *Star Trek* fan, it was a challenge not to fawn when interviewing Worf (Michael Dorn). *Photo by Lucie Aleks.*

IT'S OKAY TO BE EMBARRASSED

Everybody gets embarrassed, so it's not such a terrible thing to experience that emotion during an interview. It's only human and we are, after all, mere mortals.

During an interview with the lovely Jodie Sweetin, from *Full House* and *Fuller House*, she innocently said, "We should have dinner sometime."

I responded, "Yes, we should break bed."

I immediately turned fire engine red.

Now was that a Freudian slip or just the mistake of saying "bed" instead of "bread?" I don't know. What's important is that the audience loved it and it showed a very real, very human emotion that all of us sometimes experience. And that's nothing to be embarrassed about.

Jodie Sweetin enjoying my flub during our interview. *Photo by George Kritikos.*

WHAT IF A CELEBRITY'S NOT READY TO OPEN UP?

If you feel a celebrity is not ready to answer a particular question, the best thing to do is back off, continue creating rapport, and then try again.

Once more, it's similar to dating. If you go to hold someone's hand and they're not ready, back off, continue having fun together, and then try again.

In many ways a celebrity interview is like starting a friendship or going on a first date. The goal is to "click" with the other person.

Jeff Conaway, who starred with John Travolta in the film version of *Grease*, and who was one of the cast members of *Taxi*, was booked for an interview. I was hoping to get him to share some of his personal struggles, so I asked him how he felt about young celebrities who are dealing with substance abuse. After answering, he talked openly about his own addictions and his difficult road to recovery.

Sometimes it's easier for someone to open up if you ask questions that focus on others.

A candid interview with Jeff Conaway. *Photo by George Kritikos.*

SAVE "WOW" FOR JULY 4TH

When a novice interviewer doesn't know what to say, or isn't really listening, they'll blurt out, "Wow!" This is a lazy shortcut to reacting without asking a good follow-up question. I listened to a podcast interview where "Wow!" was said at least twenty-five times. Not even clever enough to mix it up with a "Gee!" or a "Huh!" If a celebrity says, "I have three movies coming out this year," there are an infinite number of follow-up questions. The worst thing that you can say is, "Wow!"

Dishonorable mentions:

- Really?
- Yeah?
- No Kidding!
- Yowza!

LAUGHING DURING A CELEBRITY INTERVIEW

Another common question I get is how and when to laugh during an interview. I'm sure you've seen interviewers guffaw throughout an entire conversation. It's disturbing and unnatural. It's like a fan asking for a selfie, and no matter what the celebrity says, they laugh.

I once had lunch with a TV actor and a fan came over to our table and said, "Can we take a picture together?"

And the star said, "Not now, I just got out of a hernia operation," and the fan busted out laughing. He thought my friend was trying to be funny and figured laughing was the best response.

As an interviewer, try not to do this. If something is genuinely funny to you, then yes, it's okay to laugh. However, be honest with your reactions. Don't play the role of hyena—you'll lose respect from both the celebrity and the audience. As the interviewer, your job is to listen, clarify, set up, guide, and when something strikes you as funny, by all means laugh. For examples, watch how interviewers like David Letterman, Ricky Gervais, Chelsea Handler, Stephen Colbert, Steve Harvey, and Jimmy Kimmel have handled interviews with funny actors and comedians.

It's okay to break up when someone like Leslie David Baker from *The Office* makes you laugh. *Photo by Lucie Aleks.*

SHOULD YOU TAKE A POLITICAL STANCE?

Deciding whether to publicly express your political views is a personal choice. What works best for me is to remain a neutral and non-partisan interviewer.

I once interviewed an actor on my show, and it was going great until he brought up his political views. I saw half of the studio audience shaking their heads in disagreement and then disengaging. The interview was wounded and never recovered.

Even though it was the guest, not me, who expressed a political view, I never want to divide the audience. It works well for many interviewers, just not for me. If you love the work of Sean Hannity or Rachel Maddow and want to express your political ideology, then doing that would be right...or left. Just be prepared for half the audience to go right...out the door.

HOW TO HANDLE A RAMBLER

Rambling guests can be tricky. When you have a celebrity who's rambling, and it's hurting the interview, you want to move things along without being disrespectful or disregarding what they say.

If the celebrity's with you in person, here's a simple trick. When you want them to stop talking, touch their arm in a friendly but firm way. This looks okay, even on television, and it will cause them to stop talking momentarily and you can gently switch subjects.

I once interviewed a rock star who started rambling about a football game that he watched earlier. I knew that when the interview aired, that game would be ancient history. I grabbed his arm and said, "Maybe they'll win next time. In your opinion, what makes someone a winner in life?" He shifted gears and gave a great answer that had nothing to do with football.

If the celebrity is not with you in person, don't interrupt by talking loudly over them. This not only shuts them down but also damages the rapport that you've worked so hard to build. Say something like,

"I'm so sorry to interrupt you, but our time is limited and I want to give you a chance to talk about your new movie."

This speaks to their best interest and allows them to move on without any hostility.

WHEN YOU REALLY SCREW UP

One time I was interviewing an actor from the movie *United 93,* which dealt with the heavy topic of 9/11. The actor pointed out that he looked like a terrorist and that's how he got cast in the movie, and although the part went well, unfortunately there's no more work for him.

I said, "Well who knows, maybe there'll be a sequel."

Immediately the studio audience started hissing and booing. I screwed up and knew immediately that I had to correct the situation. I stopped the interview cold and talked with the audience.

I said, "Wait a second. Do you *really* think that I'm advocating another 9/11?"

Then I walked right in front of them and said, "I agree, it was a dumb mistake, but it was unintentional." I said, "If anybody here really thinks that I want another terrorist attack on my country, you should leave the television studio right now."

I stood there and waited. No one left. I stood up for myself and was able to continue the interview. In fact, after that, every time I referred back to my idiotic mistake, everyone laughed.

When you screw up, you should immediately explain, apologize, or soften it with humor. If you don't, it will not only ruin the interview, but it can stay with you forever.

Another time, while interviewing Neil Brown, Jr., who played DJ Yella in the film, *Straight Outta Compton,* I asked where he was from.

He said, "Anaheim, California."

"Oh, Straight Outta Disneyland," I joked.

I could tell he didn't like that one bit. But I quickly apologized and explained it was just a silly joke—I didn't mean he wasn't tough or anything. Luckily, he was cool with that and we went on to discuss his being a black belt in karate and how he also trained in Wing Chun, Gung Fu, Wah Lum, Jujitsu, Judo, Tae Kwon Do, and Capoeira That quickly mended any awkward feelings, solidified his badass status, and led us to having an enjoyable interview.

Interviewing *Straight Outta Compton* actor and martial arts expert, Neil Brown, Jr.

GLORIA GAYNOR AND I WILL SURVIVE

In 2009, I interviewed Gloria Gaynor, the Grammy-winning singer of classic hits like, *I Will Survive.*

I desperately wanted her to sing that song, but on the night of her appearance, we had technical problems, so a stage performance wasn't going to be possible.

(It's important to remember that every problem has a solution.)

During our on-air interview, I asked if she would sing the song directly to me while sitting in her chair. What followed was Gloria Gaynor brilliantly singing *I Will Survive* as if I was the man who "did her wrong." While she sang, I behaved like the womanizing boyfriend portrayed in the song...and man, did she give it to me. She sang at me with such anger, passion and vindication that the studio audience cheered and gave her a standing ovation!

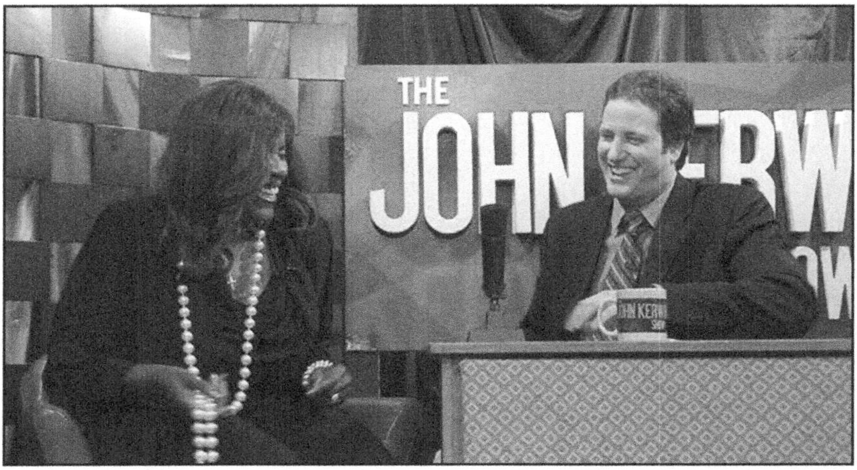

I'll never forget my interview with Gloria Gaynor...and how her song "survived."
Photo by George Kritikos.

7

MAKING YOUR INTERVIEWS EXTRAORDINARY

One way to take your celebrity interviews from satisfactory to extraordinary is to work with a coach.

Tiger Woods has a swing coach. Chess champion Magnus Carlsen has a strategy coach. Taylor Swift has a voice coach. You should have an interview coach.

My coach was Garry Shandling. Garry, of course, was a successful comedian who guest-hosted for Johnny Carson numerous times on *The Tonight Show*. He created *It's Garry Shan•ling's Show* and *The Larry San•ers Show*, and was nominated for nineteen Primetime Emmy Awards and two Golden Globe Awards. He also hosted the Grammy Awards four times and the Emmy Awards three times. On top of that, Garry was a natural at interviewing.

I would direct message him questions on Twitter about interviewing, and he always answered. Sometimes on a Saturday night, I'd thank my lucky stars that I wasn't out on a date, as Garry became available and we would message each other back and forth for hours. Here are some of the most profound pieces of advice he gave me.

"When I did interviews, it was real. It's more interesting that way. Like, 'being' not 'doing.' You only need to be."

"Your success will come from communicating consciousness, not words."

A good interview goes beyond words. **"That's where the true connection is, and from where the real unspoken communication comes."**

My questions were sometimes geared toward how I could improve my skills. Garry responded, **"You're focused on why and what to do. Stop doing anything and move into being. That is where your mystery starts. This is the focus. 'Being' is past pleasing an audience. Trust yourself to 'be.' No thought of result. Walk through that fire and you will please yourself."**

When I asked, "How do I stay in that place?" Garry responded, **"You will translate that energy when you know your full self. The false self is always measuring result. Result doesn't exist and is not your concern."**

When I would interview celebrities, my mind would always be thinking, turning, going a million miles a second. Garry explained, **"It's the strongest battle ... discipline not to think."**

I asked about the pressure to end an interview strong – like having a strong emotional moment or laugh. **"You don't need to end strong. You need to know yourself. Then you will know just what to do."**

Now, I know some of you are thinking this is very Zen, or this sounds like Yoda and is somewhat obtuse. You're right. But that aside, the message Garry wanted to convey was to be "in the moment" and honestly communicate with the other person. This is the number one lesson I got from him. Don't try to be cute, funny, or smart. Be yourself, be open to honest communication, and don't get caught up in what will be "effective" or what is trending.

Staying present is not easy to do under the pressure of a celebrity interview. At the time, I was beginning a martial arts journey and my karate master would tell me to forget technique when fighting and just "empty your mind."

Garry responded, **"Your master is 100 percent right. Become a spiritual warrior. It's a lonely path. Few are willing to commit to it. Few will understand it."**

My goal was to be a better interviewer. Garry would point out that I was, **"Result oriented, which has only abstract reality. The other is a deeper, more substantial reality which others feel."**

I pointed out my superficial issues. I was concerned with looking and dressing like an interviewer, with a ready list of professional questions. Garry told me, **"Be more and more yourself and discover what you say."**

In other words, don't be a robot and resort to prepared questions. Be present as yourself and open to discovering real moments within the interview.

He also gave me a list of books to read. If you struggle with being yourself and in the moment, perhaps they will help you, too.

The Power of Now by Eckhart Tolle

Letters to a Young Poet by Rainer Maria Rilke

The Book of Five Rings by Miyamoto Musashi

When Things Fall Apart by Pema Chodron

Zen in the Art of Archery by Eugen Herrigel

As Garry told me, **"Let whatever you're working on be your sacred spiritual place. This will automatically infuse your work. Be patient."**

Some of you may be saying, "I'd like to have a mentor, too, but I'm sure that you must've known someone who knew Garry." Not true. I wrote multiple emails to Garry's publicist, who eventually forwarded them to him. Sometime after that, Garry followed me on Twitter, allowing me to contact him privately. A few weeks after our last exchange, in early 2016, Garry passed away.

Every successful celebrity interviewer has had mentors. I've mentored many people myself, and perhaps reading this book will serve as your first mentorship. Find people in your area of interest, whose work you respect, and seek their counsel. And always remember to give back.

TALK BIG TIP

If you can't afford or find a professional coach, ask people you trust to critique your interviewing. Sometimes by simply correcting a few bad habits, your work can skyrocket from good to great.

A SECRET LETTER

If you're open to the following exercise, it can be a transformative tool, whether you're just learning to interview or you've been doing it for a lifetime.

Write out what you ideally want your subject to tell you *after* you've interviewed them. Think in terms of the highest possible level of your work.

Here's an example from when I interviewed a movie star:

> *John, I'm going to try to put into wor•s how much I appreciate being interviewe• by you. You ma•e me*

> *feel relaxed and comfortable, which allowed me to open up more than I ever have in any interview. As crazy as this sounds, our interview helped me to better realize who I really am. Throughout our cathartic conversation, I felt fully expressive, as funny and as interesting as I've ever been. Along with my film work, this interview will stand as the best representation of my essence. Together, we created a work of art that will be an integral part of my legacy. I now see you not only as an interviewer, but also as a friend.*

This exercise provides a high goal to aim for and crystallizes your intent.

TALK BIG TIP

Before meeting someone important, write out a secret letter of what you'd ideally want them to say to you, after your meeting.

ONE LINE THAT CAN BRING YOU GREATNESS

"Help me to make this the best interview of your life."

Saying that in a friendly, yet sincere way before their interview will inspire the celebrity to open up to you. They *also* want it to be the best interview of their life. Saying this shows you're going after greatness, you take this seriously, and it instantly raises the stakes, making the interview a creative team effort. It's an irresistible challenge.

ARE SOME CELEBRITIES "BAD INTERVIEWS?"

No, at least not in my experience. Any interview I've ever done which didn't go well was my fault, one hundred percent.

I didn't find the ***connection.***

I didn't find the spark to open them up.

Perhaps I failed to gain their trust.

It's never been their fault. I understand many of my colleagues will disagree with me on this, but I've seen what I thought were bad subjects give amazing interviews when handled correctly. I've interviewed accountants, tax attorneys, plumbers, real estate brokers—and all of them were interesting. Yes, even the accountants; so long as I was curious about them and followed the **Three C's.**

We all know that some celebrities are phenomenal guests, such as Sofia Vergara, Bruno Mars, Jennifer Lawrence, and Taylor Swift. They're so good, a tree trunk could successfully interview them. They're bulletproof. **Our art is to be able to conduct a *compelling* interview with the celebrity who isn't as open and needs *you* to bring out their greatness. So, for them, bring your A-game.**

THE COLD FISH

As I said, no celebrity is a bad interview. However, you might encounter a "cold fish"—someone resistant to ***connecting*** with you. It must be fixed immediately, or else the interview can turn into a catastrophe.

Right before the start of our interview, a well-known actor once said, "Just so you know, I will only be looking at the camera, not at you."

I introduced him, and sure enough, he was staring at his camera. When I asked a question, he answered directly to the camera—without ever making eye contact with me.

After he answered the first question, I said to the audience, "Let me tell you what a great film actor this man is. Before we started this interview, he told me that for the entire interview, he's only going to look at that camera and never look at me."

Still looking at the camera, the actor said, "That is correct."

I continued, "Now, while I respect his process, I really, really would like him to look at me."

The actor said, "Nope," which got a big laugh from the studio audience.

I then asked him, "Did you know that we both have the same eye color?"

He paused, and still staring at his camera, said, "No I did not!"

This got another laugh. I then got up and stood next to his camera and asked a question from there. He still didn't move his eyes even though I was only a couple of inches away from the camera lens.

So then I said, "You know what? I'm going to pick one of our studio audience members to ask you the next question."

I got a beautiful model, who happened to be in the audience, to sit at my desk. She got a lot of whistles as she made her way to the stage. She sat down in my host chair and asked him a question I gave her to read from a card. He couldn't resist and looked over at her. It got roars, which brought a big smile to his face.

At the end of the interview, he said, "I guess for television it's best to look at the interviewer."

As he was looking at me, I asked my final question to *my* camera, refusing to look at *him.* It really was a lot of fun, and the interview turned out to be one of my favorites.

Sometimes when conducting interviews, it's like you're an IT person, except instead of fixing a computer, you're troubleshooting the interview. You can't let the system crash. If the celebrity's a cold fish, turn on the heat.

WHEN THEY'RE SMARTER THAN YOU

I once interviewed Binyamin Stivi, who was one of the stars of the show, *Chil• Genius.* I'm not ashamed to say that at 12, he was a lot smarter than me. (Or is it "I"?)

Rather than compete with him, I explored his mind with questions, comparing his interests in aerodynamics theory and wanting to win a Nobel Peace prize to my interests at the same age, which included playing with a yo-yo. I even showed him an old school science project of mine, which was primitive, to say the least.

It takes practice to interview geniuses, which I had the opportunity to do at Cornell. I exercised my right as a student to have private meetings with my professors, which led to, you guessed it, me *interviewing* them. I met with some of the greatest minds in the world and, as was their nature, they were often condescending to me, the uninformed teenager. They enjoyed quizzing, testing and catching me with questions that only James Bond could answer. Like that time a super villain asked Bond if he recognized a rare species of fish. And Bond answers, "Of course… Pterois volitans."

For this type of interview, show appreciation, listen intently, then ask follow-up questions that demonstrate a high level of curiosity.

And don't be afraid to go into child mode. If you confront or challenge them, it will ratchet up their anger or shut them down. It's not in your best interest to say, "You're being rude," or "Don't condescend to me." Let your audience decide. Your job is to make the guest ***comfortable***, ***connect*** with them and do everything that you can to make the interview ***compelling***.

Child Genius **star Binyamin Stivi examines my brainless school science project of the solar system.** *Photo by Lucie Aleks.*

PHYSICAL CONTACT DURING AN INTERVIEW

As monstrous as he was, Charles Manson was a well-known public figure and was interviewed many times during his life. I've studied them all, and my favorite was conducted by Geraldo Rivera in 1988.

Unlike other interviewers, Geraldo was unafraid of Manson. At one point, Manson threatened him, but Geraldo was not intimidated. It gained Manson's respect. In fact, Geraldo physically touched him numerous times, which no other interviewer had ever done, slapping him on the arm and touching his shoulder. After they'd discussed the etched-out swastika on Manson's forehead, Geraldo put his index finger on it, jabbing at it with disdain. It was ***compelling*** and showed that Manson, in essence, was a bully who had met his match.

Contact and touching can elevate an interview. It's simply more personal.

When Jimmy Fallon messed up Donald Trump's hair during an interview in 2016, it was ***compelling***. He first made Trump ***comfortable*** and established a ***connection***, which allowed him the opportunity. Jimmy really went for it, tousling his hair into a giant mess. Some in the media criticized him, saying it wasn't professional. But I disagree, because if you want substantive, you get George Stephanopoulos, Lester Holt, or Lesley Stahl. Fallon's job is to entertain, and that moment of contact was truly entertaining.

TALK BIG TIP

Thinking about appropriate contact with the celebrity, that's never forced, is another way to help make your interviews compelling.

One time I interviewed an actress who revealed that she'd just had breast implants and was very happy with the results.

She asked me, "Would you like to feel them?" (Have I mentioned lately that this is the best job in the world?)

Of course, her request was something I'd never bring up myself, but since she asked, I agreed. She put my hand under her blouse and I turned fifty shades of red. I just stood there frozen. I was speechless.

I couldn't think of anything to say except, "This is by far the best interview I've ever done."

I've had celebrities read my palm, arm wrestle me, dance with me, ask for a piggyback ride, as well as many other forms of contact during an interview.

Oprah Winfrey will touch a guest sometimes more than twenty times during an interview. It's one way she ***connects.*** She seizes opportunities to hug, hold hands, high five, wrap her arms around them, and even cup their face in her hands.

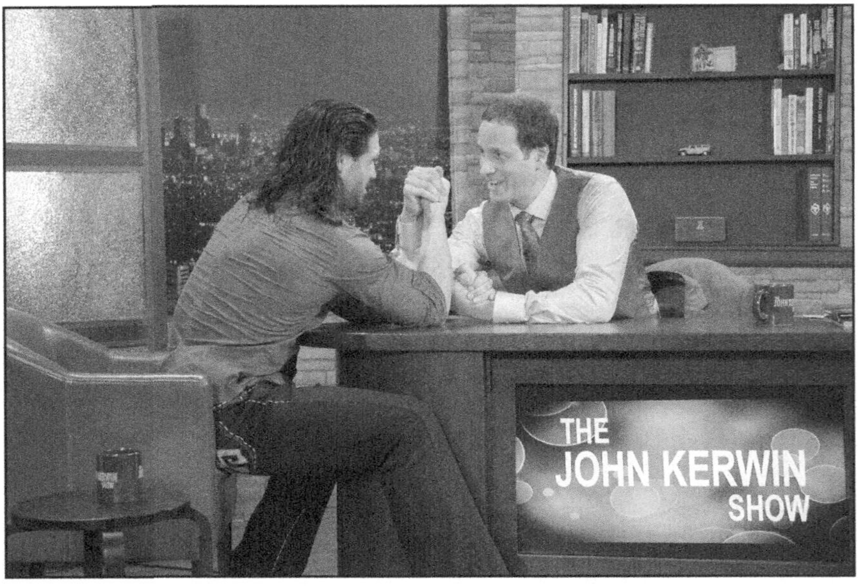

Physical contact can elevate an interview, like when I arm wrestled WWE star John Morrison. (Yes he won.) *Photo by Lucie Aleks.*

CONQUERING DISTRACTIONS

- Audio is streaming through the cameraperson's headphones
- An audience member sneezes
- The guest is wearing jewelry that keeps hitting their lavaliere mic
- A set piece falls down
- The still photographer accidentally trips
- The stage manager is flashing time cues every couple of minutes

These are just a few distractions I've dealt with during an interview. So far, I've avoided an earthquake. All the while, I have to stay in the moment, listen, follow up, keep the energy high, gauge audience reactions, ***connect*** with the guest, and make the interview as ***compelling*** as possible. It may sound intimidating, but it's a skill that comes with practice.

Staying in the moment and having a good sense of humor really helps when dealing with distractions. In fact, all those screw-ups can work in your favor if you handle them correctly. Some of the biggest laughs often come from mishaps during an interview.

One time the studio lights accidentally went out. I immediately started slow dancing with my guest, who was a comedian. He let me lead. Soon people in the studio audience also started dancing, while my audio supervisor played *Dancing in the Dark*. A momentary technical problem turned into a ridiculous dance party. The key is not to get rattled or lose your cool under pressure.

And take dance lessons, because you never know.

During a commercial break, practicing how to operate a prop while Stage Manager Dency Nelson and Producer Stacy Altman give last second notes.
Photo by George Kritikos.

AH, DON'T SAY THAT

I've been a member of Toastmasters International® for many years, and one of the best things I've learned from that public speaking organization is to remove "filler words." Filler words are unnecessary words commonly inserted between thoughts. Some examples are:

"Ah"

"So"

"Um"

"Er"

"Like"

"Y'know"

And "And"

The definition also extends to clicking your tongue, scratching your head, laughing at your jokes, and many other gestures that undermine the power of your public speaking.

The reason people use fillers is because they're naturally afraid of silence, and fillers bridge the gap of what to say next.

The truth is, pausing is far more effective and not something to fear. Great speakers and interviewers rarely use filler words. Martin Luther King Jr.'s legendary speech wouldn't be nearly as effective if he'd said, "I Ah Have a Dream."

The rare exception is when a filler word is intentionally used for comedic reasons. For example, an actress once asked David Letterman, "When was the last time you had sex?"

Dave replied, "Ahhhhhhhh."

Well, that's funny because he was using a filler word to show how he was uncomfortable and wanted to avoid answering the question. Other than that, filler words only serve as a hindrance, driving a wedge between you, your subject, and your audience.

The way to eliminate filler words is to be conscious of them in your everyday life and self-correct yourself. Listen to your taped interviews, count the fillers you hear, then slowly work toward decreasing and eliminating them.

This is a simple way to drastically improve your interviewing. It's become an obsession with me. In fact, I recently went to the dentist and as I was sitting in the chair, the dentist leaned over and said, "Say Ahhh."

I said, "I will NOT!"

WATCH YOUR INTERVIEWS

In order to improve, it's necessary to watch your work. When watching your interviews, look for things you do that distract or that take away from the effectiveness of the interview.

I used to unconsciously cover my mouth when interviewing. Covering the mouth is an instinct to protect ourselves, like when public speakers cross their arms, protecting their heart. Once I became aware of this, I worked on correcting it.

TALK BIG TIP

It helps to have fresh eyes look at your interviews and to find ways to improve. Get feedback from someone you trust.

THE POWER OF EDITING

When you read or watch an interview, you often experience only the best parts. Some journalists spend fifty hours interviewing a celebrity and then condense that down to a 10,000-word piece. The truth is, in order for someone to open up, it takes time. Even on television, interviewers often overshoot and then cut out the less interesting parts. You may have noticed this on talk shows. With multiple cameras and sophisticated editors, a celebrity interview can be cut to pieces and patched together to appear seamless. Some shows go as far as adding content during editing. In other words, if you're walking down the street talking with a celebrity, and one of the camera shots is from behind, you can add a question or a funny comment and reposition it in that spot.

I have to be careful not to give away who this is, but during my interview with a legendary actor, his dentures were falling out. You heard me right! He quickly put them back in, but unfortunately, his denture grip wasn't gripping—his chompers kept falling out.

At one point, they leapt from his mouth towards me and I found myself juggling them so they wouldn't hit the floor. Because he had such a good sense of humor about this, and was laughing, the studio audience started laughing, too. Every time he put his teeth back in, within thirty seconds they flew out again. It was like a perfectly orchestrated Charlie Chaplin routine, except this was real.

As the interview concluded, I told him, "This may have been the funniest interview ever!"

The studio audience gave him a standing ovation. He responded with his version of a mic drop by taking his teeth out and throwing them on the floor.

That night I got a phone call from his publicist, and I knew what was coming. In order to protect his client's career, he asked me to edit out all the "Dancing Denture" parts of the interview. I tried convincing him the interview would be watched by millions and would greatly help the actor's career because he handled it with such aplomb.

No dice. It had to go.

I told the publicist, "Don't worry, I give you my word, we'll edit it all out."

In fact, I went a step further—I had our audience coordinator contact every member of the studio audience from that night to tell them to keep the incident quiet. To my knowledge, they all did.

The following night, I sat in with my editor for hours upon hours. Not only did we have to fix "DentureGate", but none of my reaction shots were usable as I was almost always laughing hysterically. So my editor had to use my cutaway reaction shots from an earlier interview that night and splice them into this interview.

We also had to cut out the audience laughter as it didn't make sense. When we finally finished editing, it was daylight. We successfully retained a short, yet serviceable interview. Heartbreaking as it was, through the power of editing, we were able to keep our reputation intact.

TALK BIG TIP

The most efficient way to learn and utilize the power of editing is to sit in with professional editors as they work on your interviews. And bring coffee.

WHAT IF THE INTERVIEW WAS WEAK?

What do you do if you think the interview fizzled? Act like a professional! Don't hang your head and show your disappointment, even if it was the biggest bomb since Hiroshima. If the guest apologizes, assure them that the interview was fine and that any awkward moments will be fixed in editing. You should sincerely thank your guest, take pictures, thank their publicist, and then thank everyone on your team. Act as if the interview was a big success. Be positive. Be a leader.

Sometimes the interview may seem like a failure as it's being conducted, but then when you look at it or listen to it on tape, it may be surprisingly good.

Sometimes the reverse is true. Being positive and gracious is always the way to go once the interview is completed.

WHAT'S A LOUSY INTERVIEW?

Maybe the interviewer was trying to dominate the interview.

Perhaps they kept interrupting or asked long-winded questions forcing the celebrity to wait and wait until they could finally answer.

Maybe the interviewer was trying too hard to be funny, sound smart, or impress the celebrity.

Perhaps they lacked self-confidence, causing them to kiss up and laugh at everything the star said.

Many times, while watching interviewers, I get the feeling they're just using the guest as a straight man. That should never be done.

A long time ago, I used to do something that today is incomprehensible. I'd have comedy writers come up with funny comments I could interject during interviews. I'd be interviewing someone and just waiting for them to finish talking so I could squeeze in a joke. It was terrible, yet I still see many interviewers doing this.

I once saw a talk show host ask his guest the same question four times until he got an answer with the specific wording he needed to set-up an "ad-libbed" joke. If you're funny, allow your sense of humor to come out naturally as it would when talking with a friend.

Don't get stuck in your head. Not being "present" is one of the most common traits of a poor interviewer.

If you're thinking of your next question or something funny to say, you are not present. A good interviewer will ask a question and then discover that their next question is within the answer from the previous question, prompting a new, different question. Journalist Bill Moyers did this for hours during his excellent 1988 interview with Joseph Campbell, *The Power of Myth.*

FLIRTING

Flirting on-air with your subject can be a risky proposition. It may work for a while, and with the right chemistry, it can be entertaining, I've certainly been guilty of this. But more often than not, it gets old very fast.

Sex sells, but you need to be a really good salesman.

Sometimes, an attractive celebrity will flirt with *you.* Almost always, it's not real, they're just trying to be provocative. Plus, again, it almost always gets boring after about a minute. They say, "You're even handsomer in person," then they say, "Are you single? Are you good in bed?" Viewers watching the interview will usually roll their eyes and tune out.

What a viewer wants:

- To be entertained
- To be inspired
- To be educated
- To discover what makes that celebrity tick
- To find out what that celebrity is like as a human being
- To learn something about themselves

And once in a while, if it's done organically and it's mutual, they'll enjoy some flirting.

E.G. Daily, co-star of ***Pee Wee's Big Adventure*** and the voice of Tommy Pickles on the ***Rugrats*** examines the cleft in my chin. *Photo by Lucie Aleks.*

HOW TO GET A STAR TO RETURN

Here's how:

- If they have a positive experience
- If the final product makes them look good
- They'll also remember if you follow up to thank them, making sure to send a link to the interview
- If you use any pictures of them to promote the show, they'll remember if you got their approval, and never forget it if you don't. A picture you think is beautiful may not be flattering to them
- They might remember if you follow them on social media
- If you go to their book signings, public appearances, or charity events and politely re-introduce yourself

TALK BIG TIP

Stacking one positive experience on top of another gives you the best shot at getting a second interview.

HOW SHOULD AN INTERVIEWER SIT?

One time on television, I interviewed a celebrity while sitting with my legs crossed using the stereotypical masculine "ankle resting on the knee" position. I was amazed at the comments.

"The way your legs are crossed makes you look too competitive."

"The sole of your shoe was exposed during the interview, which was distracting."

"The way your legs were crossed, I saw above your sock and was bothered by your bare leg. I even saw some leg hair."

OH NO, not leg hair! I experimented by crossing my legs knee over knee, which, to me, always felt feminine and unnatural. But that all changed when I saw the interview—I was pleasantly surprised. I later noticed presidents like Ronald Reagan and Barack Obama sat this way, as well as almost all the best male and female interviewers.

HOW TO SAVE AN INTERVIEW

An actress who was starring in a hit television series was booked for an interview with me. On the day of the show taping, there was terrible traffic, and our studio audience consisted of three crew members. That was it. After coming out of makeup, she looked at the empty studio and said, "I'm out of here."

I responded, "Wait, give me one minute to interview you, and if you're not happy, you can leave."

She reluctantly sat down.

I started off by saying, "Today you did what our studio audience couldn't do. You made it here despite terrible traffic. How did you do that?"

She said she was already in the area because she hated traffic more than anything.

I asked her, "Why?" and she talked about how she was from the country and how big city life sucked. Her hatred for the city was deep, and it sincerely made me laugh. I kept feeding her new questions, and it became not only funny, but also cathartic for her. Once she got that comic rage out, she settled into the rest of the interview, which turned out to be one of my longest of that year.

TALK BIG TIP

If for some reason a celebrity is about to walk, stop them and sincerely say, "Just give me one minute, and if you're not happy, you can leave." Most of the time, they'll stay.

RESPECT A CELEBRITY'S SECRETS

During one interview, a celebrity was telling me how alcohol had been destroying her life, and after attending Alcoholics Anonymous meetings, she was proud to announce that it was her one-year anniversary of being sober. The studio audience burst into appause.

I then took a commercial break. The celebrity turned her back to the audience, and from her bag, pulled out a small bottle of tequila and chugged it down, inches away from me.

Moments later, I was hearing my stage manager say, "We're back in 3, 2, 1 . . ."

I stammered something like, "We're back with so and so who's just been sharing with us her victory over alcohol."

It was bizarre, but that was her secret, and it wasn't my place to bust her.

Afterward, she thanked me and said, "I'm still working out my issues. But I want you to know that anytime you want to interview me again, I'll be there for you."

I knew that as an interviewer, I had done the right thing. The truth is, you *will* experience some *Valley of the Dolls* moments when interviewing celebrities. Like me, I'm sure *you* have secrets, so respect *theirs.*

TALK BIG TIP

Off the record is a promise that something will remain private between you and the celebrity. As long as it means you won't be an accessory after the fact, never, and I mean never ever, break your word on this.

WHEN A CELEBRITY BRINGS A FRIEND, DON'T IGNORE THEM

While meeting George Clooney, who was with his right-hand man and producer, Grant Heslov, I immediately told Grant that as a boy I was a huge fan of the sitcom, *Spencer*, of which he was one of the stars. I mentioned specific episodes and how much I related to his character.

From the corner of my eye, I could see George Clooney beaming, and hanging on my every word. When I stepped away, George excitedly said to Grant, "How about that?!" He was so genuinely pleased that his best friend had gotten some attention. Soon after, George walked up to me and started a conversation, and we talked for about twenty minutes.

Sometimes the best way to ***connect*** with a celebrity is by showing respect to their friend, partner, or significant other.

CHOOSING YOUR CO-HOST

Whether if it's for a podcast, radio, or television talk show, the co-host/sidekick is one of the most complicated roles to fill. I marvel at Andy Richter's work on *Conan*. He knows when to contribute and when not to. Ed McMahon was brilliant with Johnny Carson, and I think Robin Quivers has been a huge part of Howard Stern's success. Those are the exceptions. All too often there's a natural tendency for a sidekick to compete with the host, and that can get ugly.

Personally, I've been fortunate to have my musical director, Nicholas Burns. He was someone with whom I could briefly chat and set up the show. Like Paul Shaffer on David Letterman's NBC and CBS shows, Nicholas was otherwise busy directing the house band and never sat by the desk with the celebrities.

You must have chemistry with your co-host/sidekick. You can't fake that. You can tell when a sidekick is not into the host's sense of humor or outlook on life. Sometimes a co-host will be forced on you. For example, producers may want someone younger or of the opposite sex to capture a different audience.

One famous example is the 1950s show *Broadway Open House* where the host Jerry Lester had a sidekick named Dagmar, a voluptuous beauty who wore low-cut gowns. She sat on a stool as Lester did the monologue. Not surprisingly, Dagmar got all the attention and before long, Lester quit the show. Soon after that, the show, with only Dagmar, was cancelled.

Be careful picking your co-host/sidekick and have a clear understanding of each of your roles during the show. And make sure they aren't wearing low-cut gowns.

PODCAST TEAMS

If you want to host a podcast, consider teaming up with someone with a different skill set than yours. *On Gilbert Gottfried's Amazing Colossal Podcast!* Gilbert joins forces with Frank Santopadre, and it's a terrific pairing. Frank does the research, reads the celebrity autobiographies, and writes great questions. Gilbert adds comedy, writes some questions of his own, and adds star power to the podcast.

Hotboxin' with Mike Tyson is a popular podcast where Mike talks and smokes weed with his celebrity guests. He'll often signal his well-prepared co-host, Eben Britton, to ask questions. This tag-team approach works well, allowing Mike the freedom to follow up on the answers and engage in relaxed, yet stimulating conversations.

Other successful pairings include:

- *Armchair Expert with Dax Shepard*, co-hosted by Monica Padman, who is also the show's producer
- Carolina Barlow is the co-host and one of the writers of Will Ferrell's *The Ron Burgundy Podcast*
- Sona Movsesian is the co-host of Conan O'Brien's *Conan O'Brien Needs a Friend*
- Lee Syatt co-hosts *The Church of What's Happening Now: With Joey Coco Diaz*
- Chris Hardwick's podcast, *The Nerdist,* is co-hosted by Jonah Ray and Matt Mira

TALK BIG TIP

If you have good chemistry with a celebrity, suggest that the two of you create a podcast together. If you're a good interviewer and you do the bulk of the work, the celebrity might be interested in partnering with you, and suddenly you'll have a platform with a built-in audience.

OVERCOMING DISAPPOINTMENTS

Like most things in life, there's no way to get better at interviewing celebrities without the occasional disappointment. Every interviewer, even Oprah, has had setbacks, so you'll be in good company. I was once accepted to be a correspondent on *The Tonight Show with Jay Leno*. That meant during the show, Jay would cut to me on the street interviewing people for various comedy segments.

This was going to be great for my career. However, Jay vetoed the idea. I believe he felt that choosing someone else, whose persona was goofy, weird, or dumb, would give him more to play with and help him generate more comedy on his show. He may have been right.

Oh well.

An even worse defeat was when I was in the running to replace Conan O'Brien during his move to take over for Jay Leno on *The Tonight Show*. The frontrunner for the slot was Jimmy Fallon, who not only was talented and famous, but was also friendly with Lorne Michaels, who holds great power at NBC.

Nevertheless, I was being considered and met with the brass over at the network. My only political connection was my musical director, Nicholas Burns, who'd gone to Tufts University with the then NBC

Entertainment President, Ben Silverman. Obviously, Jimmy Fallon was picked, leading to him becoming one of most popular hosts in the world.

The following excerpt is from an article entitled, "Heeeeere's Kerwin," which was featured in the industry trade magazine, *Broa•casting & Cable:*

> ***"Ever since NBC announced that Conan O'Brien would replace Leno, Kerwin and his staffers have been campaigning vigorously for consideration as O'Brien's replacement as host of Late Night . . . Still, losing out to Fallon was probably a little easier to stomach than the time Kerwin was passed over for another talk show. The winning candidate: ALF."***

That's right, in 2004, I was in the running to host a new talk show. I was told that it was between me and the 1980s puppet sensation, ALF. And ALF won.

The execs said, "If you ask ten random people on the street who they've heard of, John Kerwin or ALF, who do you think they'll pick?"

I answered, "Umm, the lump of fur and corduroy?" Adding, "How can a puppet interview a celebrity?"

They responded, "Oh, we figured that out. ALF will be at the desk interviewing guests while his creator will be hiding under the desk watching the interview on a little monitor and doing the voice."

I said, "You know, I pride myself on not being sexist, racist, or homophobic, but I think that in order to interview celebrities, you have to be human."

"We disagree."

After seven episodes, they agreed with me, and viewers, by putting the show out of its misery. However, that didn't make me feel any better. In fact, it took many years until I stopped hating puppets.

By the way, I'm a fan of shows like *Space Ghost Coast to Coast, The Muppet Show,* and *Max Headroom,* but this show was to be a real late-night talk show. In fact, they hired Ed McMahon as ALF's side-kick. To this day, I stand by my belief that for a talk show to last, the host needs to be mortal. Unless, of course, some guy flies down from Krypton.

The best way to handle disappointment is to understand there's always another opportunity around the corner, as long as you don't give up. As Sylvester Stallone wrote next to his hand and footprints at Grauman's Chinese Theatre, "Keep Punchin'!"

THE HARLEM GLOBETROTTERS

As a kid in Queens, I played basketball with my friends at Hoover Park. The trick was to make it to the courts without having the local bullies steal our basketball on the way over. If we ran into those hooligans, they'd say something witty like, "Gimme that ball or you're dead." We lost a lot of balls that way. When that happened, we were stuck playing with a tennis ball—which was really tough to dribble. Yet we still played . . . for hours and hours.

Years later, because I interview celebrities, I was asked to play on the Select Team against the Harlem Globetrotters at the Honda Center in Anaheim, California. The Select Team consisted of former college stars who were true professionals, and preparing for that game in the locker room felt like being in the NBA.

When they announced my name, it suddenly dawned on me that this was one of the highlights of my life. If you'd told me when I was a kid that one day I'd be playing basketball with the Harlem Globetrotters, I think my head would've exploded.

After the game, with the help of my producer, Don Sweeney, I interviewed some of the Globetrotters. I also signed autographs for a long line of kids. It was another example of a magical experience that came directly from doing celebrity interviews.

Walking back to my car, I noticed an old, beat-up tennis ball in the gutter. I picked it up and it became one of my favorite souvenirs.

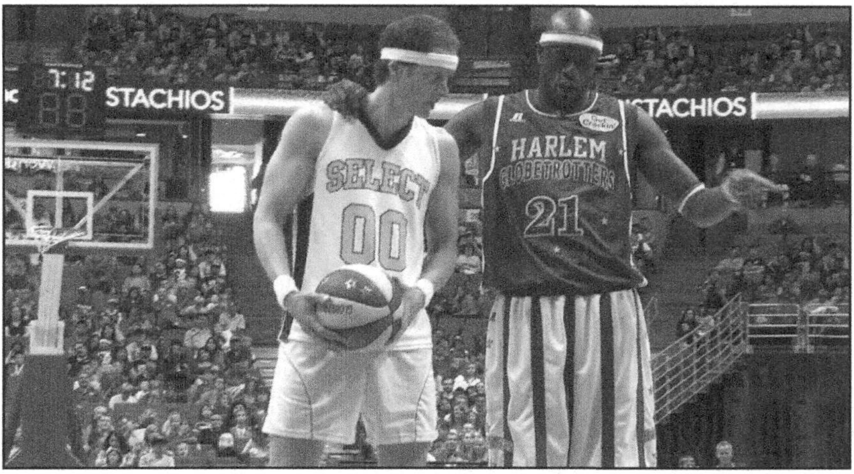

A childhood dream come true: Playing against the Harlem Globetrotters. I'm sure I don't have to tell you who won. *Photo by Don Sweeney.*

REMEMBER YOUR VICTORIES

To continue improving as a celebrity interviewer, it's important to remember your victories. This can be something as simple as booking your first interview or interviewing your very first celebrity. It may even be a compliment you receive from a star or from someone who likes your work. **Remember your victories. It will help you get through the tough times.**

The best compliment I ever received, which I still think about, came after a stand-up set I did at The Comedy Store in Hollywood. When I finished, I noticed Richard Pryor had been watching from the back. As I passed by, he asked me to bend down, as he was in a wheelchair at the time.

He whispered in my ear, "You're a funny motherfucker."

How generous was that?! And how often is "motherfucker" a treasured compliment? For me, it sure was, and it will stay with me for the rest of my life.

INTERVIEWING POLITICIANS AND COMEDIANS

Despite the glaring differences between a politician and a comedian, an interview with either one can fail for the same reason. A politician may be looking to sway voters with his rhetoric, and no matter what question you ask, they'll go into a prepared speech. A comedian may be so locked into their material that they'll use your interview to do a stand-up set. Neither are what you and viewers want.

You want your audience to get to know them as people. I've told comedians before an interview to trust me and allow me to show how they're naturally funny as human beings. When they see the value of this, they normally drop their "act" and just "talk."

Politicians are finally figuring out that the public will often cast their vote for whomever they feel most ***connected*** with, as opposed to those who just bombard them with issues and promises.

I once asked a politician, "What's your favorite movie?"

He answered, "Well I don't like violent films because violence in America is a serious problem. Those movies desensitize us into thinking that violence isn't so terrible."

I felt like saying, "Shut up and just say *Jaws.*"

Having some laughs with comedy club headliner, Maz Jobrani. *Photo by George Kritikos.*

THE WORST CELEBRITY INTERVIEW IN HISTORY?

I have to say that the worst celebrity interview I've ever seen was with Jerry Lewis in 2016. He was one of the funniest men to ever live—but he wasn't laughing during this interview. Now you have to understand that Jerry had done thousands of interviews throughout his career and if he sensed that you were either unprepared or in any way disrespectful, watch out!

It was near the end of his life and something clearly upset him. He decided from the start to only give one-word answers while looking on with utter disdain.

The mistake is that the interviewer didn't try to turn things around. Instead, he kept reading from his list of questions. The torture went on and on until Jerry finally said, "Okay, take your stuff and get out of here."

In its own way, it was so terrible it was interesting.

That interview could have been saved in an infinite number of ways. I would have stopped everything and said, "Look, Mr. Lewis, if my attitude coming in upset you, I'm sorry. I have enormous respect for you, and if you give me a chance, you will see that I did my research and I really want to help promote your new movie. If you want, you can punch me."

Then I'd close my eyes while wincing and wait. If that didn't work, I would have gone into my pocket and said, "Even better, here's my Swiss Army knife. Would you feel better if you stabbed me?"

This would have interrupted his pattern of anger and given him an opportunity to be funny.

That contentious interview could have morphed into something positive and wonderful. The interviewer just needed to be braver. (Or read this book.)

THE DANCING ALONE INTERVIEW

Speaking of bad, here's perhaps my biggest pet peeve. It's this new trend of celebrities being interviewed without an interviewer. The star sits in an expensive chair and talks about their films, seemingly alone, in a photography studio or "on set." The celebrity is well-dressed, there's great lighting, makeup...everything except an interviewer!

It's a way to save money, and from the celebrity's viewpoint, the camera's always on them and there's no threat of a crappy interviewer. I get it. Except this can never be a great interview, cause it's not an interview. It's the star rehashing stories, which they've told countless times.

I saw one of these with Al Pacino. I could almost hear someone off-camera yelling, "*The Go•father*!"

Then Pacino said something like, "Let me tell you about *The Go•father*."

Next, I could imagine someone yelling, "*Scarface*!" Then he told anecdotes about *Scarface*. There was no discovery, no byplay and no chance for a real moment.

It was worse than being interviewed by ALF.

WILLIAM SHATNER

Remember when I said it's important to find the celebrity's spark? Well, I've made my fair share of mistakes in that department. For example, I once booked William Shatner for an interview. Now Bill loves horses—it's one of his passions, so he made it known that he specifically wanted to talk about horses. I explained to his people that I'd be happy to do that but I'm a Star Trek fan and also wanted to talk about that show and its subsequent movies.

The next day he cancelled. And he was right to do so. I made a colossal mistake.

Do you think William Shatner was excited about discussing Star Trek for the billionth time? Of course not. His "spark" was horses.

I should've become obsessed with learning about horses. I could've eventually asked a bridge question like, "What would horses be like in space?" This might've gotten him to talk about Star Trek. In fact, had I been genuinely curious about horses, I can almost guarantee that he would've "given me" Star Trek anecdotes.

Now every time I see William Shatner on television, I think about how I blew that interview. Don't make the same mistake I did.

A few months after that missed opportunity, actor/choreographer Cris Judd was interested in being interviewed, but explained that he wouldn't talk about his ex-wife, Jennifer Lopez. Instead, he wanted to discuss his show, *I'm a Celebrity . . . Get Me Out of Here!*

This time around I said, "Fine, no problem." I interviewed him and we talked about the show and all the interesting things about his life and career. Then *he* started talking about J-Lo!

When a star emphatically says they want to discuss a pet project, they're basically handing you their spark. If you allow them to express their passion, and then become passionate about it yourself, more often than not they'll surprise you with their generosity.

DON'T COMPARE YOURSELF WITH OTHERS

I have a friend who once interviewed Bill Murray and then got rather depressed after seeing Bill being brilliantly interviewed by David Letterman. I explained, "You have to understand that over the course of his career, Bill Murray has been interviewed by Letterman 44 times. You interviewed him once."

Sometimes people don't consider the tremendous amount of rapport built up over multiple meetings. It's tough to compete with that.

When I interview a celebrity a second or third time, it only gets better. They trust me. They're familiar with how I interview and feel like they can be more open and playful. We have a solid *connection*.

You can learn a great many things from watching other interviewers. Don't beat yourself up because you feel that their work is better. There are many ingredients that go into a successful interview. One of them is time.

INTERVIEW WITH A VOLLEYBALL

When a guest cancels, don't panic. See it as an opportunity to be creative. When I was starting out, I remember a guest cancelled and I was trying to figure out what to do. The week before, I'd watched the movie *Cast Away* on DVD, so I asked a production assistant to go to a sporting goods store and buy a volleyball. Turns out, they even sold one with the red face printed on, just like "Wilson" from the movie. We taped a lavalier mic on "Wilson," and I interviewed him.

My introduction was something like, "I'm very excited to introduce tonight's guest. You, of course, know him from his work in the hit movie *Cast Away*. Please welcome, Wilson!"

It was very silly. I asked questions like:

"Do you think you'll be nominated for Best Supporting Actor at the Academy Awards?" (Of course, there was no answer.)

Then I responded, "I get it, you don't want to jinx it."

I asked, "Is there someone special in your life?"

(A large pause ensued.)

"Ladies and gentlemen, it's so refreshing when a celebrity, for once, doesn't kick and tell. Good for you, Wilson!"

On it went. I actually got more attention for doing that interview than I would've if the real celebrity guest showed up. I got write-ups in local newspapers, and they always wanted to know about the "Wilson interview."

It was inspiration born of crisis.

And Wilson was way funnier than the sword from *Gla•iator.*

INTERVIEW WITH A DOG

If you thought *Interview with a Volleyball* was odd, here's something perhaps even odder that will further illustrate the principles in this book.

On the red carpet with man's best friend. *Photo by Lucie Aleks.*

Interview programs often maintain a list of backup guests. For example, Drew Carey was always a backup guest on *The Late Late Show with Craig Ferguson.* Drew worked out of the same studio hosting *The Price is Right* and was always happy to stop by in case one of Ferguson's guests canceled. My backup guest was Lola the Dog.

When a celebrity canceled, Lola was my go-to replacement. I would give an on-air plug to the movie and TV animal renting company which brought Lola, one of their "stars," to the studio. However, instead of interviewing her trainer, which was the norm, I instead directed my questions to Lola. As she entered the studio, the play-on song was Elton John's *The Bitch is Back.*

Here's how the **Three C's** came into play. For ***comfort***, I had a soft cushion on the guest chair that Lola liked very much. It also served as a newspaper in case something unexpected happened. In my pocket, I made sure to have a variety of Lola's favorite treats.

I ***connected*** with Lola by petting her and rubbing her tummy, which she loved.

How was the interview ***compelling***? Well Lola did tricks, such as high-fiving, ringing a jingle bell, yawning when I told a joke, and if I shot her with an empty squirt gun and said, "Bang!" she'd turn around, limp away and then play dead. Lola would always get big applause and then, of course, she'd humbly bow.

The **Three C's** work, even when interviewing a dog.

DANCING WITH THE STARS

Accessing your "inner hustler" makes your interviews better. I was scheduled to do a sit-down interview with Anna Trebunskaya, one of the professional dancers on ABC's *Dancing with the Stars.* I was told that for the interview, Anna wanted me to promote her business, the You Can Dance Studio in Hermosa Beach, CA.

I said, "Of course, but wouldn't it be an even better endorsement if I could actually go to her dance studio and have her teach me to dance

Dancing with the Stars' **Anna Trebunskaya can make anyone look good on the dance floor.** *Photo by George Kritikos.*

as she would on *Dancing with the Stars*? We could do that dance as part of the interview."

Her people agreed, and I went to her studio. Anna taught me a cha-cha dance and we successfully did that as the culmination of our interview. Aside from pulling my groin, it was a great experience. For an entire week, I kept an ice pack on my groin, and when anyone asked about it, I'd say, "Anna Trebunskaya did this to me."

CELEBRITIES WHO SPEAK WITH AN ACCENT

Some interviewers tell me they prefer not working with celebrities who have hard-to-understand accents. That's ridiculous, and a big mistake. The goal of a celebrity interview is to create ***comfort***, to ***connect***, and to be ***compelling***—there's nothing in that statement that says, "Must speak perfect English." Everyone can relate to talking with someone who has an accent or whose second language is English. To me, this gives the interview an interesting dynamic.

I once interviewed Charo, the flirtatious Spanish-American actress and flamenco guitarist. At one point I said, "Charo, I can't understand a word you're saying."

She answered back, "No, you just misconscrew me."

The studio audience erupted in laughter.

Another time I interviewed Chuy Bravo, the little person who was the sidekick on Chelsea Handler's show, *Chelsea Lately*. Now, I happen to be a white guy who's 6'3". Yet, as physically mismatched as we were, we had a wonderful ***connection*** and the interview was very funny. In fact, for weeks afterward, we were in discussions about potentially doing a show together. When a celebrity has an accent, it just becomes another element of the interview. Would you really turn down interviewing Jackie Chan, Penelope Cruz, or Arnold Schwarzenegger? Not to mention my fellow New Yorkers Ray Romano, Cyndi Lauper, and Leah Remini.

I'd interview Quasimodo if he had a new movie coming out.

Photo by George Kritikos.

Photo by Lucie Aleks.

If anything, celebrities who speak with an accent will only enhance your interviews. Charo and Chuy Bravo were both amazing guests.

YOU CAN'T BE IN A BAD MOOD

One of my worst interviews was with June Foray, an incredibly talented voice actor responsible for the cartoon characters Rocky the Flying Squirrel and Natasha, from *The A•ventures of Rocky an• Bullwinkle an• Frien•s*; Granny in the Tweety and Sylvester cartoons; Lucifer, from Disney's 1950 movie *Cin•erella*; and hundreds of other characters. Our failure to ***connect*** was entirely my fault.

The day of the interview, I was recovering from the flu, my car had broken down, and the night before, my girlfriend broke up with me. I was in a lousy mood. On top of all that, there were audio problems in the studio and the interview was delayed. I started fuming. Although I attempted to hide it, June sensed my mood and must've been thinking, "What's this guy's problem?"

I powered through the interview, but there was little rapport between us, and I lost the opportunity to properly ***connect*** with this legendary woman.

Like a professional athlete during a big game, or a Broadway actor on opening night, you have to train your mind to block out anything that interferes with doing your best work. I'm still haunted by that interview, but it taught me a valuable lesson. Since then, I've had all kinds of annoying things happen on interview day, yet I've always shown up in a great mood.

HANDLING CRITICISM

Criticism is unavoidable. It's part of the game. If your interviews are light and fun, you'll be labelled a softball interviewer. If your interviews are more investigative, searching for buried truths, you'll be classified as an ambusher. As you gain experience, let instinct be your guide as to what works best. Don't try to be someone you're not, in order to please others. That never works.

Like him or not, Piers Morgan knows who he is. He'll never be Larry King, nor does he want to be. Discover who you are, and when you get criticized, understand that without exception, it's something every interviewer goes through.

Unfortunately, sometimes criticism gets personal. After one of my first celebrity interviews, someone online commented that I was a "five head." Do you know what that is? It's not a "forehead." It's a five head.

I told my mother, "Someone called me a five head, which means I have a really big forehead."

She said, "So...I'm the one who suffered."

STAND UP FOR YOURSELF

Occasionally, a celebrity tests you. Don't fall apart. You must believe you're their equal, not their stooge.

One time I asked a guest something and he said, "That's a lousy question." Now when starting out, I might have answered, "You're right. I'm sorry, that was a bad question. I promise to make the next one better." That kind of answer tells the celebrity they can push you around.

My more recent answer was, "I disagree. Why do you think it's a lousy question?"

He gave his response, which I challenged, and soon after he said, "Actually, it's not such a bad question after all."

He was testing me. By standing your ground, you gain respect and have a better chance for the celebrity to ***connect*** with you.

THE HIGHEST LEVEL OF THE CELEBRITY INTERVIEW

Discovery is the highest level of interviewing. Bar none. Because... not only does the celebrity discover something about themselves, you discover something about yourself.

This is what makes the Frost/Nixon interview so ***compelling.*** Through his questions and follow-ups, David Frost discovered bravery within himself and was able to turn a non-committal Richard Nixon into considering his actions and the effect they had on the American people. He gave Nixon the opportunity and the *desire* to provide the public with not only an explanation, but also an apology. After the interview, both interviewer and subject experienced a catharsis. You felt it changed both of their lives.

I believe all truly great interviews contain this element of discovery. The best way to get there is to work on the ***Three C's*** – ***comfort*** the celebrity, ***connect*** with them, and do all you can to make the interview ***compelling.***

Beyond that, you also have to go into the interview *wanting* discovery. It's like how, once in a blue moon, you go to a movie and you're just open to it affecting your life. When the movie delivers, it's a transcendent experience. This same revelation can happen in your interviews. Before the interview, picture being totally relaxed, in the moment, and open to discovery. Visualize this for every interview you conduct. This gives you the best chance to achieve greatness.

JERRY SEINFELD

Everyone, at some point, asks themselves the question, "What do I want to do with my life?" Years ago, I asked myself that question, night after night, in the most unlikely of places.

I was working as an emcee at the Hollywood Improv comedy club. Instead of merely introducing the comics, like the other emcees, I always took the opportunity to interact with them from the stage. I suppose my teenage interviewing shenanigans gave me the courage to do what others wouldn't dare try.

One time I asked Robin Williams to come onstage and do improv with me. It was an exhilarating, unforgettable experience. Afterwards, Robin rushed over to me, excitedly going over what worked and how my improvising can be improved. Those around us were in awe as this megastar was talking with me, and with such animation. Turned out, improv was his "spark."

The best "interview," however, was the night Jerry Seinfeld made a surprise appearance. As I was about to introduce him from the stage, I noticed he was wearing the biggest, most beautiful watch I'd ever seen.

Onstage I asked, "Jerry, can you tell us how much that watch cost?"

From the corner he shouted back, "I'll tell you how much this is, if you tell me how much that piece of shit *you're* wearing is."

Everyone laughed.

Then I asked, "How about coming up here and switching watches with me for a moment?"

So Jerry Seinfeld walked on stage and we switched watches. As soon as I put on his enormous watch, I immediately fell to the floor, because it was so heavy. Jerry put on my watch and walked around like he was going to get a skin disease because my watch was so cheap. The audience loved this.

After we gave each other back our watches, I said, "That was great! Now can we switch cars?"

Well that night a producer was in the audience. He came up to me after the show and said, "You should be interviewing celebrities. And I'd like to help you."

And that's how my career began.

Remember, "A.B.I. – Always Be Interviewing."

CONCLUSION

Writing this book has been a maddening experience. I once read that Picasso would work on a painting for years, always looking to improve it. Finally, when it was hanging in an art gallery, he'd walk up to it and start working on it some more. I can see myself in a bookstore with a pencil writing in new anecdotes. (You remember bookstores, right?)

Some final tips and reminders:

A.B.I. – Always Be Interviewing. Whether it's your Uber driver or your dental hygienist, make it a daily practice to interview people.

Implement the ***Three C's: Comfort, Connect, and Compel***—those are the keys to a good interview.

Stay on top of celebrity culture. Read *People* and *US Weekly* and follow *TMZ, E! Online*, and other sites.

Become a social media maven by following celebrities and other interviewers on Twitter, Instagram, and Facebook. Read celebrity autobiographies and familiarize yourself with their official websites for content and trends. Watch celebrity interviews on YouTube, and listen to podcasts and radio, and watch TV interviews. Whenever possible, attend live studio tapings and read celebrity interviews transcribed in book form.

Concentrate on the type of interviewing you want to do. When watching or reading an interview, note what you like and don't like. Ask yourself what, if anything, is ***compelling*** about the interview. Then ask yourself, "How would I have made it more ***compelling***?"

Make contacts in your specialized area of celebrity interviewing. Offer free services, and intern at local stations or podcast studios. Learn the craft while getting ***connected*** with people who are working toward similar goals.

The formula for mastering celebrity interviews is:

1. *Interview as often as you can.*
2. *"Direction and Correction" Use a qualified coach.*

These two elements, combined with a burning desire, will lead to mastery.

Make interviewing a way of life. You're embarking on a journey to discover a passageway to Hollywood royalty. Your life will be enriched, bringing you a highlight reel of mashed-up "super moments" that will redefine your world.

People have asked me, "I'll bet you'd like to interview Sylvester Stallone again." The truth is I wouldn't. Meeting him that first time was so powerful, I wouldn't want to diminish that which has served my life and career so well. It's like when, at fifteen, I read *The Catcher in the Rye*. Nothing can compare to that life-changing first reading. I never read it again, and never will.

Sylvester Stallone showed me that my dreams were possible. And I want you to know that your dreams are possible. Go after them, and then keep going after them.

Oh, and watch out for Cloris Leachman.

APPENDIX A

THE TALK BIG INTERVIEW CHECKLIST

Interview preparation varies depending on whether it's conducted by phone, video conference, in a podcast studio, at the subject's home, or in a television studio. Follow this outline to secure and create successful celebrity interviews.

- ☐ Find your interview subject. Write letters and emails, go to autograph shows, and research direct contact details for local celebrities.
- ☐ Prepare for the interview by thoroughly studying the subject's work, social media, YouTube videos, and websites.
- ☐ Use a focus group for ideas on what your audience wants to know about the guest.
- ☐ Ask friends and relatives what they want to know. Keep improving your list of questions.
- ☐ Think of how the interview can be as ***compelling*** as possible.
- ☐ Utilize their talent/skills during the interview.
- ☐ Write out a secret letter on how you envision the celebrity reacting to the interview. Read it again before the subject arrives.
- ☐ Prepare your questions and do all that you can to avoid using notes. But have them on hand in case they're needed.
- ☐ Research the location. If possible, go on a test run to see that it's quiet and is an acceptable place to conduct an interview. Have your recording device charged and ready.

- ☐ The week prior: Email reminders to the subject with date, time, location w/directions, and your contact information EACH TIME.
- ☐ Mentally prepare to be in the best mood possible and understand there may be obstacles to overcome (guest is late, bad weather, location needs to be changed). Part of your preparation is having backup plans.
- ☐ Arrive at least 15 minutes early. If you're not waiting there to greet them, at best you'll lose an opportunity to create ***comfort***, at worst, they'll bail.
- ☐ Assign a person to be ready to take pictures of you after the interview (usually tipping a host or food server will make for a dependable photographer).
- ☐ As soon as the subject arrives, turn off your phone.
- ☐ Greet subject (perhaps with a gift) and immediately work on ***comfort*** and ***connection***.
- ☐ Casually mention you've started taping.
- ☐ Remember the Three C's: make the guest ***comfortable***, ***connect*** with them and make the interview ***compelling***.
- ☐ Find the guest's "spark."
- ☐ If there are no time restraints, wait for the subject to end the interview. You want as much time and footage/audio as possible. Remember: the longer the interview, the better the chances to ***connect*** with the subject and bring out the most ***compelling*** moments possible.
- ☐ Once finished, sincerely thank the subject. Keep the recording device on. If some new and interesting dialogue occurs, ask the subject if you can use it.
- ☐ After asking for the subject's permission, have your assigned person take pictures of you and your guest. Try and get at least ten pictures,

with different poses, if the guest is willing.

- [ ] Give a sincere, warm goodbye, and promise to email the finished product and to keep them updated.
- [ ] Immediately write notes for yourself on your impressions of how the interview went.
- [ ] Review your secret letter and see how it matches up against the actual interview. Consider how future interviews can bring you closer and closer to your optimal level of excellence.
- [ ] Celebrate your victory!
- [ ] Send a follow-up thank you email to the subject and keep them up to date on when they'll receive a link to the final interview. Ask for their approval on all photos, which should first be edited to look their best.
- [ ] Support the celebrity in their endeavors (book signings, screenings, social media) to keep the relationship alive. (And to get a second interview as well as referrals to their celebrity friends and colleagues).
- [ ] Book your next interview. Rinse, repeat, and keep getting better!

APPENDIX B

TRANSCRIPT OF DAVID CARRADINE INTERVIEW WITH COMMENTS

Earlier in the book I mentioned my favorite interview was with the actor David Carradine. This interview took place relatively early in my career. David was a boyhood hero of mine, and getting the chance to interview him was surreal and thrilling. You'll notice how the interview demonstrates many of the ideas I've covered in this book. Comments were added to complement the text, to explain what I was thinking during the interview, and to show how preparation was essential. I hope you get the opportunity to interview your heroes. There's nothing like it.

January 2007
LOS ANGELES, CA; *"The John Kerwin Show"*

John Kerwin: Tonight's first guest is a true icon. You, of course, know him as the star of *Kung Fu*. As a leading man, he starred in films such as: *Bound for Glory*, *Death Race 2000*, Martin Scorsese's *Boxcar Bertha*, Ingmar Bergman's *The Serpent's Egg*, *Gray Lady Down*, *Circle of Iron*, *The Long Riders*...I'd keep going, but I want as much time with him as possible. His new book is *The Kill Bill Diary: The Making of a Tarantino Classic as Seen through the Eyes of a Screen Legend*. Please welcome, Mr. David Carradine!

COMMENT: Giving a thorough, well-deserved introduction builds *comfort* and *connection*. Taking the time to memorize this lengthy introduction showed that I admire and respect his body of work. As a backup, and a good trick to remember is I had the introduction taped onto the back of his book. As I held it up, I could glance at the introduction, if needed, without David or the audience knowing.

(Audience applauds.)

John: Strong handshake! That's exactly the handshake I would have expected from David Carradine. Thank you for coming on the show. You're staring at me like you want to kill me. *(Pause)* Do you enjoy turning on the intimidation?

COMMENT: Remember to begin in the moment. Perhaps to establish dominance, he intentionally shakes my hand very hard, so it makes sense to call attention to that. Big issue right out of the gate: he seems to be very wary of me. I'm not panicking, but I'm definitely aware that I must confront and diffuse this.

David Carradine: I never turn it on. It just kind of happens.

John: Well it's not necessary tonight. I'm here to honor you.

COMMENT: I make the decision to overtly confront any suspicions or preconceived notions that he might have of me, right away. This is my first interview with him, and he's probably had many bad interviewing experiences in his career. It's my job to get him to trust me.

David: Glad to hear it. Thanks for this. *(David takes out the bottle of champagne which I gave to him as a gift backstage.)* Let's drink.

(Audience applauds as he opens up the bottle.)

COMMENT: It's rare for a guest to bring out the gift that I left for them backstage. But it's a great choice on his part. As I've written, gift-giving can help your interviewing in many ways.

John: I'm not a big drinker. I may not be able to interview you properly.

David: That's good! I don't want to be interviewed properly.

(David pours champagne into my mug.)

John: Just a drop.

(David continues to pour, filling John's mug to the brim.)

John: When.

John: When.

John: Whenever.

(John raises his mug.)

John: Here's to me blowing my most important interview!

David: I'll drink to that.

(They drink. David downs the champagne from his mug in one shot, smiles at John and then fills it up again.)

John: You can really drink! Did you drink with Tarantino on *Kill Bill*?

COMMENT: Sensing the comedy moment of drinking is over, I change directions by *connecting* drinking to his films.

David: We drank a lot. Quentin is a really good drinker. He surprised me.

John: He could knock it back, huh?

David: He sure can.

John: I read that in your book, ***The Kill Bill Diary***, which I loved by the way.

David: Thanks.

John: And I believe that you're the only person who could get away with writing this type of behind the scenes book. It includes personal letters that you wrote to Quentin, private conversations. For example, one night you were smoking cigars with Quentin and talking about the mythology of Superman and, soon after, it was turned into one of the most memorable scenes of the movie.

David: Well we talked about alter egos, Clark Kent, Peter Parker. Anyway, six days later a rewrite of the script came out and Quentin turned that conversation into one of his delightful non-sequitur monologues.

John: Three things made that happen. One: casting David Carradine. Two: having long, one-on-one talks with you socially. And three: taking the essential parts, skillfully rewriting and perfecting them and then integrating them seamlessly into the film. Brilliant!

David: Quentin's a mad genius and those monologues are at the heart of all of his movies.

John: I also love how in ***The Kill Bill Diary*** you dissect the difference between Quentin and other directors. For instance, you write how Steven Spielberg understands violence, or at least knows how to show it. Quentin, on the other hand, understands violent *people*.

David: Yes, he understands what's inside them.

John: One of my favorite parts of the book is when you describe, in detail, the scene from ***Kill Bill*** where you make a sandwich for your daughter BB next to Uma. We get an inside glimpse into not only your acting skill but also Quentin's directing.

David: I must've made a hundred sandwiches for that scene.

John: Well let's make it a hundred and one!

(Audience applauds as John takes out sliced turkey, bologna, cheese, mustard and bread. It's all spread out on the desk. Then he then hands David a huge, razor sharp chef's knife.)

(David laughs and goes to work making a sandwich.)

David: I made sure to wave this knife around a lot in the scene…to be menacing.

John *(Ducking and holding his hands up):* Effective!

David: Perla, who played my daughter, likes the crusts off the bread, which gave me more things to do with the knife.

(David gives John the finished sandwich.)

David: There ya go!

(John eats half the sandwich and gives the other half to an excited member of the studio audience.)

John: Is it true that you didn't have prior experience with samurai swords?

COMMENT: Reading your subject's book is one the best things that you can do. In preparation for this interview, I also read David's autobiography, *Endless Highway*.

David: Well, yes, that was a new thing for me. It was in ***Kill Bill*** that I got interested in samurai swords. Look at the old series—they would never let me use a weapon, never. I had to do empty hand. I had some weapons, the Chinese weapons. There is a thing called the Nine Sectional Whip which is really… they also call it the chain whip and it was like that thing that the Hell Angel's haul out and smack you with. Anyway, I learned how to use it. I can do shoulder rolls and stuff and swing it around you know and just everything.

John: What do the movements with the chain whip look like?

(David gets up and mimes the intricate movements of the chain whip.)

(Audience applauds.)

COMMENT: Always look for opportunities to have the subject demonstrate their skills. It adds entertainment value to the interview. (See Chapter 5, "*Show Me The Talent!*")

John: That was terrific!

David: I know, but the Executive Producer said, "Yeah but what are you going to do with it?" And I said, "Well use it, use it in the show." He said, "We can't have you using a weapon." So I never got around to learning the samurai sword until I started training for ***Kill Bill*** and I fell in love with it. And also, you know I was on the wires. You know the wires?

John: Yes, like in ***The Matrix***.

David: Can you imagine flying through the air swinging a Samurai Sword? That's fun!

John: I wish we could do it right now. But we don't have the space…or the insurance. However, I did bring something. On both ***Kung Fu*** and in ***Kill Bill*** you play the flute, also called the silent flute. I got my hands on this classic instrument. Considering that it's been sterilized, would you mind playing something?

David: Of course.

(David expertly plays the silent flute.)

COMMENT: Another chance for David to entertain, by displaying his musical talent on an instrument he played in his iconic roles.

(Audience applauds.)

David: I brought a flute, similar to this one that I got from ***Kung Fu***, one of many I have, and I brought it onto the set of ***Kill Bill.*** One day Quentin saw me playing it and decided to put it in the movie.

John: And it fit perfectly. By the way, I gotta tell you my absolute favorite TV show growing up was ***Kung Fu***.

(Audience applauds.)

John: So many people loved it. Is it true that you patterned your speech for Caine after Mr. Spock from ***Star Trek***?

COMMENT: This question came from my research and when I ran it past a focus group, as *Star Trek* fans, they said it was a question they were very interested in.

David: It was supposed to be a secret, John! Well there are certain similarities between the two guys, right? Caine and Spock.

John: Well they both talk deliberately.

David: They talk deliberately, they're both kind of strangers in a strange land and they're both incredibly ethical, right? They've both got this certain strangeness you know.

John: Otherworldly… especially Spock. And to emphasize that stranger in a strange land, you would go onto the *Kung Fu* set without reading the script and not knowing what the scene was about.

David: I'd look at the script for only a minute or so. It really worked. I had no idea what the story was about. *(Audience laughter)* It's like I was dropped from another planet. I never told anyone, particularly the directors. They'd freak. *(More laughter)*

John: Would you mind saying something as Kwai Chang Caine?

David: *(As Caine)* Would you like some more champagne?

(Audience laughs and applauds.)

John: *(Laughing)* That's not something you'd expect to hear from Caine.

COMMENT: It's a risk asking him to talk as Caine from *Kung Fu*. However, I feel like we're now *connecting* and it's worth trying. If he'd said, "No," I was prepared to talk as Caine myself and ask him to critique me. That may have induced him to correct me and then talk as Caine.

David: *(Looking into the audience and the workers on the set.)* You're a very interesting dude.

John: Me? Why do you say that?

David: Ya got all these people working for you. How did you get them to all come out here?

John: The same way I got you.

(David laughs.)

John: Lots of champagne! I heard there was an incident backstage between you and one of our crew members.

David: You heard.

John: Apparently one of our guys made the mistake of asking, "Do you really know kung fu?" And you lifted him up by the throat, off the ground. My producer was panicking thinking there would be a lawsuit, but Tad over there was thrilled! He ran into my office to show me your handprint on his neck.

COMMENT: I didn't plan on bringing this up, but when David pointed out the crew, it came to mind. It also gave the audience an inside peek into some backstage hijinks, which luckily turned out fine.

David: He's okay. I didn't hurt the dude. You should take up taekwondo.

John: Yeah? I took karate as a boy, but it was too expensive, and I had to stop at yellow belt.

David: Taekwondo would be good for you because you're very tall and there's a lot of kicking, it gives you an advantage on reach and distance. I studied a lot of tai chi for the series.

John: Speaking of ***Kung Fu***, is it true that the part was originally created by Bruce Lee for himself, but the producers felt that he was, "Too short and too Chinese?"

David: No not really. In the first place he had nothing to do with the creation of it. A guy name Feldman wrote the script, a New Yorker who was studying kung fu and I think the script—if you understand what the story is about—which is a Caucasian who is allowed into the Shaolin monastery…well that already throws Bruce Lee out.

John: Right, because he's Chinese. This is great that you're clearing this up. There's been a lot of debate over this.

COMMENT: That's my way of encouraging him to amplify his answer.

David: Well I'm clearing it up now! This writer dreamed of being the only Caucasian, right. So he wrote this script and it found its way eventually into Warner Brothers, it was like—it sat there for six years and then this guy Jerry Thorpe who was the executive producer, and I would call him the creator of the ***Kung Fu*** series, he'd seen me doing a play on Broadway where I played Atahuallpa in ***The Royal Hunt of the Sun*** and I was really built up; it was a very athletic part and I was pretty much in a loin cloth most of the time and I actually stole the show from Christopher Plummer. I was the toast of New York and then five years later Jerry Thorpe found this ***Kung Fu*** script and the first thing he said was, "This is an excuse for me to hire David

Carradine." Now when you've got a project like this from Warner Brothers, the news spreads around fast and Bruce Lee heard about it and said I want to audition for it. So they brought him in for an audition. And he didn't get it. I got it! ME!

(Audience applauds and cheers.)

COMMENT: I thought that for history, it was important to finally set the record straight. Books have been written about this and, to this day, there's still a lot of controversy over who created *Kung Fu* and if it was originally Bruce Lee's role. I'm glad it was cleared up... at least from David's perspective.

John: You have a bunch of movies coming out.

David: Well I made six last year.

John: Which are your favorites?

David: Well, my favorite is a movie called ***Camille*** which has James Franco and Sienna Miller in it and was produced by Al Ruddy.

John: From ***The Godfather.***

David: ***The Godfather, The Longest Yard,*** and ***Million Dollar Baby.*** He's just one of these old guys, you know. I like that movie a lot. Another one I like is a caveman comedy. It's called ***Homo Erectus.*** It's not dirty. A whole bunch of films coming out.

John: *(Pause)* Y'know, I want to tell you that you've had quite an impact on my life. You were my boyhood hero, you starred in the first and the best, martial arts TV show ever. And then you starred in, what I believe...is the greatest martial arts film of all time, ***Kill Bill.*** *(Applause)* And, in between, you've had, and you continue to have, a terrific body of work. You're a great actor, a man's man and the fact that you'd come on this little show means the world to me.

(Audience applauds.)

(David shakes John's hand.)

John: You didn't shake it as hard that time.

David: Well now we're friends.

COMMENT: There's always the danger that complimenting a guest can come across as flattery. But in this case, it's genuine. I'm glad I was able to say that to him.

John: *(After a long pause)* Now, I hope this doesn't bother you, but I'd like to try something *(Crowd laughs)* that would be a great thrill for me. On ***Kung Fu*** there's the scene when Master Po would say, "Snatch the pebble from my hand," and if you could do it, you were ready to leave the monastery. Now, I happen to have a pebble right here *(Audience cheers)* and I was wondering if you'd like to try and snatch the pebble from my hand?

David: Okay!

(Audience applauds.)

COMMENT: I never cleared this idea with David, which is intentional. Planned bits with guests often end up looking...planned. There was a chance he'd say no, but he doesn't. Turns out David gives me more than I ever expected.

John: So that everyone understands, I have a pebble in my hand. I will hold my palm out with the pebble showing and then David will try and snatch the pebble from my hand before I close it.

David: Right.

John: And I'm very fast. *(Pause)* Are you ready?

David: Ready.

(Silence as David and John look at each other. John holds out his palm with the pebble exposed.)

(David goes for the snatch and John quickly closes his hand.)

David: Show your pebble.

(John opens his hand. It's empty.)

(Audience applauds.)

(David shows the pebble.)

John: There it is!

(Audience cheers.)

David: Do I get to keep it?

John: Yes, that's one of the few things in our budget.

(David smiles at John.)

David: Your turn.

John: My turn?

(David holds out his palm showing the pebble.)

(Audience cheers.)

John: Okay.

(Another moment of silence. David and John lock eyes. John reaches for the pebble as David shuts his hand.)

(John opens his hand and can't believe that he got the pebble.)

(David smiles broadly.)

(Audience applauds.)

David *(Quoting from Kung Fu)*: It is time for you to leave.

(Audience laughs and cheers.)

John: Normally, that would be a great ending. *(Audience laughs)* But I want this interview to be truly special.

David: Now you *are* being like Quentin. He would never stop until he got a scene the way he wanted it.

John: Because we love making celebrity interviews!

(David laughs.)

COMMENT: This is an inside joke as Quentin is known to do extra takes and then yell to the crew, "Because we love making movies!"

John: What's the meaning of life?

(Audience laughs.)

John: I'm serious.

David: *(After a long pause)* Well, I'll tell you what I think. My favorite book is Ouspensky's ***In Search of the Miraculous***, which tells us that we're all dreaming. We wake up in the morning from one dream into another. I think we're all living in a little box. We think it's the world, but it's just a box. If we work hard, really hard, we break out of the box, and find ourselves in a truly big, wide world. But if we continue to evolve, we'll eventually discover that this New World is just a bigger box. And then, maybe, we'll break out of that one into, yes, another much bigger box. The process may be endless. I don't know. I may not live long enough to find that out. But if there's no end to it, it doesn't matter how long I live, or how many times I reinvent myself, I'll never come to an ending to the journey.

(Audience applauds for over thirty seconds.)

John: See, I knew we weren't done. Thank you so much for joining us. This is the book, ***The Kill Bill Diary.*** David Carradine!

David: See you in the movies.

Connecting **with David Carradine led to a compelling interview.** *Photo by George Kritikos.*

100 CELEBRITY INTERVIEW QUESTIONS

Warning: Do Not Use These Questions

Your questions should come from your own brain and be specific to the celebrity whom you're interviewing.

The questions should be based on the extensive research you've done and by what's happening during the interview, in the moment.

That said, use the following to stimulate your mind and to help you come up with your own questions. Notice they're short and clear, which is important because a long, convoluted question will confuse your guest and the audience.

But seriously, if the situation fits, by all means, help yourself to these.

1. Do you remember the exact moment you decided to become an actor/singer/dancer/author?

2. What event from your childhood has stayed with you most?

3. Are you comfortable listening to/watching your work?

4. When you first became a star, what was the first expensive thing you treated yourself to?

5. What's been the biggest surprise since becoming famous?

6. Do you remember your first job?

7. What has stardom meant to you?

8. Were you a good student?

9. Who's been your favorite leading man/woman?

10. Did you ever imagine you'd be this successful?
11. If you weren't in show business, what would you be doing?
12. Who in your field do you most admire?
13. For young people watching, what advice would you give if they wanted a career like yours?
14. How does your family feel about your career?
15. Is there a dream role you haven't done yet?
16. Who's someone you'd like to work with?
17. How would you describe your sense of humor?
18. Who makes you laugh?
19. What was it like working with (Name)?
20. Do you believe in love?
21. Is it difficult for a celebrity to find romance?
22. What do you look for in a relationship?
23. What's the last video game you've played?
24. What the biggest misconception about you?
25. How has your life changed in the last year?
26. Are you someone who saves or collects things?
27. What's your all-time favorite book?
28. What's the last TV show you binge-watched?

29. Do you find that you were happier before or after success?

30. What kind of food do you like?

31. What's a hidden talent that you have?

32. Do you believe in fate?

33. Do you believe in love at first sight?

34. What sacrifices have you made for your career?

35. Is luck a factor in a Hollywood career?

36. Is your life as glamorous as some people think?

37. What's something about you that might surprise people?

38. What would you do differently if you started your career today?

39. Would you want your children to go into show business?

40. What are you most proud of?

41. Do you cry watching sad movies?

42. What's the closest near-death experience you've had?

43. Do you have any fears?

44. This is a tough business; how have you handled rejection?

45. What are your feelings about social media?

46. Do you like to dance?

47. What was your favorite TV show as a kid?

48. What did you say when asked, "What do you want to be when you grow up?"

49. Do you remember your first kiss?

50. When people come up to you in the street, what do they say?

51. What's the oddest fan request you've ever had?

52. Who's your celebrity crush?

53. What makes you angry?

54. Are you superstitious?

55. Is there something that you've always wanted to do during an interview?

56. When was the last time you got into a physical fight?

57. Who, in your mind, is a genius?

58. Do you have a temper?

59. What's one of your pet peeves?

60. What do you do when you need to relax?

61. How did you learn about sex?

62. What's a movie you can watch over and over again?

63. Do you hold a grudge?

64. What's your best sport?

65. Do you sing in the shower?

66. What does happiness mean to you?

67. What was the greatest moment of your childhood?

68. What's your favorite place in the world to visit?

69. Are you a dog or a cat person?

70. How would you describe your bedroom?

71. Do you like to gamble?

72. How does your personality change when you drink?

73. Do you like Los Angeles?

74. Would you say that you're an optimist or a pessimist?

75. Do you ever talk to yourself?

76. Do you remember the first joke you told as a kid?

77. If you go on a date, what's a deal breaker for you?

78. If you talk with someone who's smarter than you, do you get intimidated?

79. Do you speak any other languages, or do you want to?

80. What do you think happens when we die?

81. Are you someone who's always on their cell phone?

82. If you had to cook for someone, what's your best dish?

83. Are you a morning person or a night owl?

84. What do you not have enough time for?

85. What's the last video that made you laugh?

86. If you had to do karaoke, what song would you sing?

87. If you had to change your name, what name would you pick?

88. What's on your bucket list?

89. Do you like surprise birthday parties or hate them?

90. What's your best board game?

91. Are you competitive?

92. What's a movie most people like, but you hate?

93. What was the last concert you went to?

94. Have you ever been on a dating app?

95. Do you remember your first phone?

96. Who do you think is the greatest athlete of all time?

97. What food do you hate and will not eat?

98. What's your favorite gadget you own?

99. What's the most embarrassing article of clothing you own?

100. How do you feel you've made the world a better place?

BIBLIOGRAPHY

In the 4th grade, my class was tested on what we learned during a visit to the school library. One question was, "What's the difference between a biography and a bibliography?"

I answered, "A biography is a book about someone who's famous. A bibliography is about someone who's not."

My teacher marked my paper with a big red X, with the comment, "Nice try."

Below is a list of books that have helped me become a celebrity interviewer.

Alba, Ben. *Inventing Late Night: Steve Allen an• the Original "Tonight Show."* Prometheus Books, 2005.

Apatow, Judd. *Sick in the Hea•: Conversations About Life an• Come•y.* Random House, 2015.

Battaglio, Stephen. *Davi• Susskin•: A Televise• Life.* St. Martin's Press, 2010.

Cavett, Dick, and Porterfield, Christopher. *Cavett.* Harcourt Brace Jovanovich, 1974.

Douglas, Mike. *I'll Be Right Back: Memories of TV's Greatest Talk Show.* Simon & Schuster, 1999.

Fallaci, Oriana. *Interviews with History an• Power.* Rizzoli Universe Promotional Books, 2016.

Frost, David. *I Gave Them a Swor•: Behin• the Scenes of the Nixon Interviews.* William Morrow, 1978.

Golson, Barry G. *The Playboy Interview.* Putnam Adult, 1981.

Grobel, Lawrence. *The Art of the Interview.* Three Rivers Press, 2004.

Gross, Terry. *All I Di• Was Ask: Conversations with Writers, Actors, Musicians, an• Artists.* Hachette Books, 2004.

Kelley, Kitty. *Oprah.* Three Rivers Press, 2011.

King, Larry, and Gilbert, Bill. *How to Talk to Anyone, Anytime, Anywhere: The Secrets of Goo• Communication.* Gramercy, 2004.

King, Norman. *Donahue: The Man Women Love.* Lorevan Publishing, Inc., 1989.

Leamer, Laurence. *King of the Night: The Life of Johnny Carson.* William Morrow & Co., 1989.

Lipton, James. *Insi•e Insi•e.* Dutton, 2007.

Lucas, Ed, and Lucas, Christopher. *Seeing Home: The E• Lucas Story: A Blin• Broa•caster's Story of Overcoming Life's Greatest Obstacles.* Gallery/Jeter Publishing, 2015.

Paar, Jack. *P.S. Jack Paar.* Doubleday, 1983.

Rader, Peter. *Mike Wallace: A Life.* Thomas Dunne Books, 2012.

Wenner, Jann, and Levy, Joe. *The Rolling Stone Interviews.* Back Bay Books, November 1, 2007.

Index

POST-INDEX SCENE

When I enjoy a movie, I always stay until after the credits, hoping for a post-credit scene.

Since you're still here, hopefully you've enjoyed my book.

Here's the post-index scene.

Years ago, I'm driving in Los Angeles and the car in front of me is a gold Mercedes with the personalized license plate, IKE TURNER. I think, "It can't be! But if it is, maybe I can ask him for an interview."

So I speed up and pull next to the car at the next red light.

Sure enough, it's him.

He stares at me and says, "That's right, bitch, I'm Ike Turner!"

I'm speechless.

It was one of the rare moments in my life when knew better than to TALK BIG.

TALK BIG TOOLBOX

The perfect companion to *Talk Big*

Going through my files, it occurred to me that there would be great value for readers to have access to my personal documents and correspondences relating to celebrity interviews.

These letters and documents have consistently worked, and draw on years of trial and error. And you can cut and paste them, then tailor them for your needs.

The *Talk Big Toolbox* has over a hundred pages of:

- Emails to celebrities and publicists that secured guest bookings
- Sponsor outreach
- Follow-up notes, editing notes, staff notes, focus group questions
- Question lists for specific celebrities
- Post-interview critiques
- Effective wheeling and dealing strategies
- And much more!

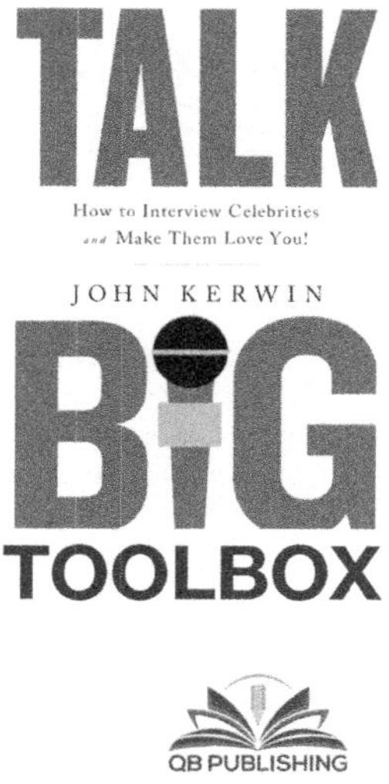

All designed to make your life as a celebrity interviewer far easier and more successful.

The *Talk Big Toolbox* is a digital book that can be purchased on **JohnKerwin.com**

Made in the USA
Coppell, TX
31 August 2023

21011138R10134